# CONCE...
## worldwide

Concern Worldwide is Ireland's leading aid agency. Last year Concern marked 40 years of working in the developing world. Today we are based in 28 of the poorest countries around the world where we are playing a significant role in improving life standards for those in great need.

When it came to marking our fortieth anniversary we made a point of not considering it a celebration. How could we, since our work is far from done. But we passionately believe that we are moving on the right road and that we are playing a significant role in improving the living conditions of those with whom we work.

Concern places immense importance on working with local communities, local societies and their governments.

We listen to the very poorest people. They know more about poverty, disease and discrimination than anyone else. Armed with that knowledge and their wisdom we undertake long-term development work and also respond to emergency situations as they arise.

Concern campaigns at both local and international levels for the rights of the hungry and destitute. We try to give the poorest of the poor a voice, knowing that justice on a global level demands that their voice be heard and appreciated. Anything less is simply not acceptable.

# DEAR PRESIDENT OBAMA ...

## The Concern Worldwide 2009 Writing Competition

*Edited by*
Michael Doorly

The Liffey Press

Published by
The Liffey Press
Ashbrook House, 10 Main Street
Raheny, Dublin 5, Ireland
www.theliffeypress.com

A catalogue record of this book is
available from the British Library.

ISBN 978-1-905785-65-0 (pbk)
ISBN 978-1-905785-69-8 (hbk)

Illustrations by Hillary Goudie

Supported by the EU

Printed in the United Kingdom by Athenaeum Press.

# Contents

## Part 1
### JUNIOR CATEGORY
### (12–15 years old)

# Contents

# Contents

## Part 2

### SENIOR CATEGORY
### (16–18 years old)

## Passages, Extracts, Quotes

Aisling Toner .................................................................. 117

Sierra Weir ................................................................... 118

David O'Sullivan ........................................................... 119

Megan Sweeney .............................................................. 120

Emma Delaney ............................................................... 121

Carolina Salinas ............................................................ 122

Hannah McDonnell ......................................................... 123

Sophie Rogers ................................................................ 124

Oliver Glover ................................................................. 125

Eoin O'Driscoll .............................................................. 126

Brigid Leahy ................................................................. 127

Nicola Pepper ................................................................ 128

Jessica Zamora .............................................................. 130

Eibhlin Browne .............................................................. 131

Maura Naughton ............................................................ 132

Daniel Clancy ................................................................ 133

Jennifer Gargano ........................................................... 134

Michael Magee ............................................................... 136

Gerard Mullane ............................................................. 137

Jessica Leen .................................................................. 138

David O'Keeffe ............................................................... 141

Leia Valenzuela .............................................................. 142

Jackie Lara ................................................................... 144

Rebecca Keating ............................................................ 145

Kenny Adeyima .............................................................. 146

Emily Rutherford ........................................................... 148

Mary Anne Lambert ........................................................ 149

Suzanne Ni Fhionnain ..................................................... 151

Carla Sunderman ........................................................... 153

Tammy Oruwariye .......................................................... 154

Jacklyn Nagle ............................................................... 155

# Part 3

## ADULT CATEGORY

### (over 19 years old)

# Contents

# Acknowledgements

Concern expresses its sincere thanks to all those who sent in "letters" to this year's competition for the time and effort, passion and energy with which they addressed the issues of World Hunger, Climate Change and Child Labour.

Our thanks are also due to the many people who served as first round judges for their diligence and hard work in reading each and every entry, not just once but twice, and in so doing ensuring that every letter was given the best possible chance of reaching the final stages.

Our distinguished panel of final round judges included Fr Aengus Finucane (former CEO of Concern), Deaglán de Bréadún (*Irish Times*), Gary Murphy (Dublin City University), Kelly McShane (Concern US), John J. O'Connor (Board Member of Concern US), Chris Elliot (Guardian Newspapers) and Fr Ciaran Kitching.

We have endeavoured to make this a paper-free competition (except for this book of course) by insisting that participants send in their entries by email only. That it worked so well is due in no small part to the Concern IT team consisting of Vincent Richardson, Barry Gildea, Ellen Ward and Janette Strickland.

Our media partner, *Hot Press* magazine, helped bring the competition to a whole new "socially aware and activist" audience as evidenced in the large number of entries we received from those in our 19+ age category. In creating such a fruitful partnership, we express our thanks to Brian Kearney, Mark Hogan and Paul O'Mahony.

*Acknowledgements*

Finally, to the Active Citizenship team in Concern, particularly Lucy Deering, Evanna Craig, Derval O'Brien and Grainne O'Brien, for coordinating the many strands of the competition from its earliest inception to the production of the book you hold in your hands.

# Tom Arnold

*Message from the Chief Executive of Concern*

Young people want, or should want, to change the world. And the world has changed to an almost unimaginable degree over the past 50 years.

One indicator of the scale of that change is the election of Barack Obama as President of the United States. When he was born in 1961, the political struggle for civil rights was still at an early stage. That was two years before Martin Luther King gave his famous "I have a dream" speech at the Lincoln Memorial in Washington, spelling out a vision of the future which, in those days, seemed a distant possibility.

Today, his dream has not yet been realised: injustice, inequality and prejudice continues to exist in the US, as in every other country in the world. But the election of Barack Obama shows that at least part of that seemingly impossible dream can be realised.

Progress has been made in eliminating world hunger, in abolishing child labour and in combating climate change, however we need that dream and inspired leadership to achieve these goals. We need intensely practical targets to work towards them, a step at a time. We need the current generation of young people to demand political change.

Some of us also have a dream that great inspiring ideas can be expressed in simple clear language. Texting and the world of instant communication make it more difficult to achieve this. But the essays in this book show that it can be done.

This book is Concern's small contribution to retain the "audacity to hope", to quote President Obama, that one day "all God's children, black and white, Jews and Gentiles, Protestants and Catholics", to quote Martin Luther King, can both dream and write about their dreams to the standards shown in this book.

*Tom Arnold is Chief Executive of Concern Worldwide.*

# Michael Doorly

*Preface*

The Concern Cecil Woodham Smith Creative Writing competition was launched as one of a series of events marking the 40ᵗʰ anniversary of Concern in 2008 when we invited both students and adults to reflect on some of the big issues of our time that directly impact on the developing world.

The competition is named after Cecil Woodham Smith, an Anglo-Irish author, who in her books on the Great Irish Famine, the Crimean War and Florence Nightingale reflected on issues relevant to Concern's work today: deprivation, politics, conflict and humanitarian assistance.

In our inaugural year we invited entrants to project themselves 50 years into the future and to imagine their grandchild had just asked them to recall, "what was the greatest human achievement in your life time", and without skipping a beat you replied, "why that was the year they ended world hunger". The task for those brave enough to take up the "pen" was to tell us how hunger was finally defeated.

We were both delighted and surprised to receive over 600 entries from points far and near. The eventual winners received their prize from the former United Nations General Secretary Kofi Annan at the International Hunger Conference hosted by Concern.

In this our second year we caught some of the *Yes We Can* spirit by inviting entrants to let us know what they would write in a letter to President Obama on one of three critical issues: World Hunger, Child Labour or Climate Change in the Developing

World. Once again we were delighted to receive over 800 "letters" from countries as far-flung as Liberia, Australia, Niger, Pakistan, Japan, India, as well as the United States, United Kingdom and Ireland.

More than the quantity of letters however was the quality of the words contained therein. While quick to congratulate President Obama on his historic victory, they were equally as quick to remind him of the monumental tasks that awaited him. Figures from history, past and present, were brought out to remind the President that "a hungry man is not a free man", or that "no easy problems come to the President", and "where a person lives should not determine whether they live". While he may never have the good fortune of meeting those who have entered this year's competition, he will do well to listen to their counsel and advice.

We have reproduced in full the winning and short-listed letters and have included edited extracts from over 100 other entrants. It is our hope that by presenting a copy of this book to the United States Ambassador to Ireland, His Excellency Dan Rooney, it may eventually find its way into the hands *and heart* of President Barack Obama.

### Announcing the Concern Cecil Woodham Smith Creative Writing Competition 2010

In 2010 the United Nations Secretary General is summoning a meeting of world leaders, and he is inviting YOU to address them. The 3rd annual Concern Writing Competition will invite students to submit the speech they would deliver to the assembled gathering. Keep an eye on www.concern.net/writingcompetition for all details commencing January 2010.

*Michael Doorly is Head of Active Citizenship at Concern.*

# Deaglán de Bréadún
*Foreword*

It is at least arguable that the support of the late Senator Edward Kennedy was crucial in ensuring the victory of Barack Obama in the race for the White House last year. No doubt the Senator's elder brother, John FitzGerald Kennedy, would have approved and been no less pleased to see the ultimate prize in US and, indeed, world politics going to an African-American.

Many comparisons have been drawn between Presidents Obama and Kennedy. There are obvious similarities of style and approach and, possibly because of the Irish connection, they were both gifted with remarkable eloquence.

Among the many phrases in JFK's inaugural address that can still stir the blood was his appeal to "Ask not what your country can do for you, but what you can do for your country".

A similar appeal to selflessness was made by President Obama when he said, after taking the oath of office, "To the people of poor nations, we pledge to work alongside you to make your farms flourish and let clean waters flow; to nourish starved bodies and feed hungry minds. And to those nations like ours that enjoy relative plenty, we say we can no longer afford indifference to the suffering outside our borders, nor can we consume the world's resources without regard to effect."

Napoleon said that "The moral is to the physical as three is to one" and the world needs inspiring leadership if it is to deal effectively with the pressing and inter-related problems of hunger and climate change, not to mention other issues such as child labour.

In that spirit, it was encouraging to note the enthusiasm and originality of the essays submitted for the Concern Worldwide 2009 Writing Competition. In an age when commentators lament that we have turned into an economy instead of a society, it is heartening to see that the generation now coming forward has, if anything, greater awareness of the world's problems than their elders.

Congratulations are due to Concern for organising the competition as part of its great ongoing project to combat hunger and deprivation in the developing world. In these days of cutbacks and budget restrictions, the more that can be done to raise awareness, the better, and these essays are a most laudable contribution in that regard.

*Deaglán de Bréadún is Political Correspondent with* The Irish Times *and author of* The Far Side of Revenge: Making Peace in Northern Ireland. *He served as a final round judge for the 2009 Concern Writing Competition.*

# Human Chain

## By Seamus Heaney

Seeing the bags of meal passed hand to hand
In close-up by the aid workers, and soldiers
Firing over the mob, I was braced again

With the grip on two sack corners,
Two packed wads I had worked to lugs
To give me purchase, ready for the heave

The eye-to-eye, one-two, one-two upswing
On to the trailer, then the stoop and drag and drain
Of the next lift. Nothing surpassed

That quick unburdening, backbreaks's truest payback,
A letting go which will not come again,
Or it will, once. And for all.

*Nobel Laureate Seamus Heaney has been a long-term supporter of Concern and is a patron of Concern US. Reprinted with permission of the author.*

# Part One

# JUNIOR CATEGORY

## (12–15 years old)

**An extract from President Obama's Inaugural Address, January 20, 2009**

To the people of poor nations, we pledge to work alongside you to make your farms flourish and let clean waters flow; to nourish starved bodies and feed hungry minds.

And to those nations like ours that enjoy relative plenty, we say we can no longer afford indifference to the suffering outside our borders, nor can we consume the world's resources without regard to effect. For the world has changed, and we must change with it.

...Our challenges may be new, the instruments with which we meet them may be new, but those values upon which our success depends, honesty and hard work, courage and fair play, tolerance and curiosity, loyalty and patriotism – these things are old.

...What is demanded then is a return to these truths. What is required of us now is a new era of responsibility – a recognition, on the part of every American, that we have duties to ourselves, our nation and the world, duties that we do not grudgingly accept but rather seize gladly, firm in the knowledge that there is nothing so satisfying to the spirit, so defining of our character than giving our all to a difficult task.

This is the price and the promise of citizenship.

# First Place – Junior

## Eoghan Curran
*Northern Ireland, Age 14*

**Subject:** WORLD HUNGER

Dear Mr President,

My name is Eoghan Curran and I am a 4th year student at Aquinas Grammar School in Belfast, Northern Ireland. I was delighted when you were elected President of the most powerful country in the world and thrilled also to see you join in the St Patrick's Day celebrations in the White House. Your country has played such an important part in the peace process in Ireland and clearly you plan to continue your involvement with us.

Another important issue in the world today is the amount of hunger that people experience. Back in 1963 a predecessor of yours, John F. Kennedy, set himself two goals: firstly that a human being would walk on the moon and secondly, that world hunger would be a thing of the past by the end of the decade. The first was achieved almost 40 years ago, the second goal remains as distant as ever.

There are many reasons why world hunger remains a huge issue, some of which we have little or no control over, such as drought. However, there are a number of things that we can control and that is what I would want you to focus your energy on during your presidency. Firstly, everyday debt repayments take much needed resources from developing countries so that when a country is hit by drought it is unable to cope with the resulting famine. Debt cancellation does work – in 10 countries that have had debt cancellation, spending on health has increased by 70%, spending on education increased by 30% and there has been no increase in military expenditure. Bono, lead singer with the Irish group U2, has called on western countries to cancel debts of third world countries to help them develop their hospitals, schools and industry.

Armed conflict violates the right to food by destroying crops, food stocks, livestock, homes and farms. It would cost approximately $30 billion every year to eliminate starvation and malnourishment in the world, yet in the year 2000 alone world military spending came to a total cost of $1,500 billion. Another great Irishman, Bob Geldof, who headed Live Aid for Africa in 1984, raised over $60 million for famine relief. Global spending on the arms trade is $60 million every 20 minutes, much of this in the USA.

I know there are things that our own government also has to do, particularly in relation to the Common Agriculture Policy (CAP). European agricultural policies cause hunger in the developing world because their subsidies mean that European food is sold on world markets and in developing countries at less than it costs to produce, undercutting the world's poorest farmers. This is an issue that is currently under review and hopefully changes will be put in place that will mean a fairer market for everyone.

Sometimes governments put in place policies due to pressure from the west to pay back debts that in turn cause famine to occur. An example of this was in Ethiopia during the famine of 1984. Some of the best farming land in that country was being used to grow animal feed to export to Britain and the rest of the world so that they could generate income to pay off part of their debt. An older example happened in Ireland during the Great Famine in the nineteenth century when over one million people died and two million people emigrated at a time Ireland remained a net exporter of food.

Issues such as these need great world leaders to show example to everyone else. I think that you are one of the great leaders that can show the world the true benefits of change by cancelling world debt and reducing spending on arms and military. You are inspiring a new generation of young people, you have the power and I believe you have the will, please help the poorest in our world.

Looking forward to seeing you in Ireland soon.

Many thanks,

Eoghan Curran

# JOINT SECOND PLACE – JUNIOR

## Anna Lyttle
*Northern Ireland, Age 15*

### Subject: CHILD LABOUR

Dear Mr President,

Children are bought and sold, like you might buy a bar of chocolate, smuggled across borders like your children might sneak a cookie from the jar, forced to wake in their shanty town or shop doorway in the early hours to labour while your own children are tucked up soundly in their beds. Child labourers stand for endless hours sowing stitch after stitch, fighting on the front line or working from dawn to dusk in the tobacco fields. For these injustices there are no comparisons. In another life these could have been your children ... no doubt you will thank God they are not!

Your first job, I believe, was as an ice cream scooper in Baskin-Robbins, Honolulu. You said it was the worst job you ever encountered, "your wrist got sore", and the ice cream was just so hard. Of course you had the choice to take this job and could leave when you desired. Could you imagine your seven-year-old daughter, Sasha, working from dawn till dusk every day of the week scooping ice cream? This particular job doesn't seem very demanding, but you would not ask your daughter to do it.

So many of the global population don't have a choice; no matter how much they thank God and pray, their families need money. They need food and water and shelter ... all the things we expect and don't think twice about. They have no choice but to send their children to work, or even more horrifically, this choice is taken from them in the middle of the night.

Mr Obama, I ask you to imagine waking in the morning, rousing your children for another day at school … but they've gone, disappeared, left no trace. You're puzzled and confused, not knowing what has happened or where they could have gone. Could they have been taken? Captured? Could they have got out? No! Not your children, because you have a big front door with a strong, secure, unbreakable lock, cut off from the dangers of the outside world. But the parents of these unfortunate children do know exactly what has happened; they've had the burden of this worry on their shoulders from the day their child was born. Children are trafficked all over the world. No doubt you thank God that every morning you wake up and hear your children call 'Good morning, Daddy!'

Surely no parent would sell their child under any circumstances. Try to put yourself in the situation where you would even consider selling your child or giving your child away. It's impossible, yet parents of developing countries in the twenty-first century feel they have no choice. We find it hard to believe … just say no, we think. But life is so bad at home they may very well believe they are better off involved in trafficking. Better off herded into a cramped stuffy truck with hundreds of others in the same situation leaving their families, communities, everything and everyone they have ever known, and not certain they will ever return to see their families again. Mr Obama, I ask, can you even start to imagine, conjure up even the slightest feeling of the excruciating pain that these parents and children go through?

We hope, we want to believe, we feel we know for sure … no parent would ever choose to make their child a Child Solider. Brainwashed, forced to fight, forced to kill, given guns the size of themselves and put on the front line. But they have no choice. It's do or die. Over 300,000 children, worldwide, as young as five, have been forced to leave home to live in camps and be taught to kill.

And girls … used as sex slaves or sold on for prostitution, exploited for adult perversities on an everyday basis. So young and naive, so innocent like any child, like your children! They have no idea what is going on. This is everyday life and they know no better. It's unimaginable. No doubt you thank God for your children's innocence, love and the carefree world they belong to.

We can't begin to understand how hard life is, not just physically but mentally, emotionally, for these child labourers; children not fully grown, ignorant of the outside world and completely lacking in protection and education. Your children won't start thinking about jobs for at least another eight years and only then if they choose, but these children don't make the choice, they don't even get the chance. No doubt you thank God every day that your two children have the right to make their own educated decisions and choose the life they want to lead.

No doubt you look at your children every day, loving everything about them from the top of their heads to the tip of their toes; every line, every flaw, every inch of skin, the smoothness of a cheek and softness of tiny delicate fingers. Could you let those very things become a reason to let your child go? Their vulnerability increasing their chances of getting more money on the street and their tiny fingers so small they can sow the football for your back garden or the sweater for your back better than you can. "Nimble fingers", they're said to have, "perfect for the trade". Or is it just that their wages are lower and there is less chance of them putting up a fight?

Yes. no doubt you look at your children every day, loving everything about them from the top of their heads to the tip of their toes. No doubt you thank God every day for their priceless perfection.

Anna Lyttle

# JOINT SECOND PLACE – JUNIOR

## Eoin Ferry
*Ireland, Age 15*

**Subject: WORLD HUNGER**

Dear President Obama,

I am a 15-year-old Irish student, and I am writing this letter to you to express my feelings on an issue that claims the lives of millions of innocent people every single year. Hunger is one of the biggest problems that we as a world community have to deal with. By this time next year, four million people, the equivalent to the entire population of Ireland, will have perished because of starvation. In my view, this cannot be accepted by the privileged Western World. We simply cannot allow our less fortunate brothers and sisters who are wasting away to continue living their lives in constant suffering.

Are you hungry? I wouldn't think so. Neither am I. And however much we might complain of being "starving", we cannot begin to comprehend the true horror of continually having empty stomachs. There is an Irish *seanfhocail*, an old saying, which reads *"Ní thuigeann an sach an seang nuair a bhíonn a gíoll féin lán"*, which means, "The well fed do not understand the hungry when their own stomachs are full". This saying, although ancient, still is very relevant in today's society. Allow me, Mr Obama, to put the vast divisions between rich and poor into perspective for you. The average American earns $32,140 per year. Contrast this with the paltry earnings of the average Ethiopian – $108. In 1984 this figure was $190, and it is clear from these figures that the wealthy North is not doing enough to correct this terrible injustice. There are 1.2 billion people in the world that are hungry. Similarly, 1.2 billion people in the world are obese. We in the West do not know what it is to see our siblings, parents, children or friends die from malnourishment, and to be powerless to help them. The Universal Declaration of Human rights states that:

"Everyone has the right to a standard of living adequate for the health and well-being of himself and of his family, including food, clothing, housing and medical care and necessary social services, and the right to security in the event of unemployment, sickness, disability, widowhood, old age or other lack of livelihood in circumstances beyond his control."

I ask you, Mr Obama, as the most powerful political figure on the planet, how can we quote this Declaration when, every day, it is made redundant, when two-thirds of human beings do not have enough food to survive? How can we turn a blind eye to these appalling statistics? How can our consciences allow us to sit by and watch as the dignity of our fellow man is destroyed?

The causes of world hunger are many, varied, but not undefeatable. To understand the magnitude of this problem, we must understand its roots. Overall, a shocking $38 billion worth of food is thrown away every year. The direct cost of hunger and malnutrition is estimated at $30 billion each year. Most of the widespread hunger in a world of plenty results from deeply rooted poverty, and also waste and ignorance on the part of the rich nations of the world. Land is distributed extremely unfairly, with tobacco industries diverting huge amounts of lands from producing food to produce tobacco. Since when did cigarettes become more important than food?

Also, causes of the considerable shortage of food in the less developed areas of today's world can be traced to specific events: droughts or floods; armed conflict; political, social and economic

10

disruptions; natural disasters; conflict; poverty; poor infrastructure and over-exploitation of the environment. As well as the obvious sort of hunger resulting from an empty stomach, constant hunger can make people vulnerable to numerous diseases and increase the risk of premature death. This can be as a result of a lack of medical help which we, in the developed world, can and must provide to these poor countries.

I urge you, Mr Obama, to use the power that you have earned to rectify this crisis. In your inaugural address, you told the world, "To the people of poor nations, we pledge to work alongside you to make your farms flourish ... to nourish starved bodies and feed hungry minds." As I am sure you are well aware, if you can fulfil this promise, and considerably reduce world starvation, you will be deemed one of the greatest American presidents ever, a title which I am certain you are determined to strive to achieve.

Some people think that only by giving a small donation to Concern or other humanitarian organisations they won't be able to make any difference. But this is the wrong attitude; every little thing done can help, but the third world needs a larger number of people doing this "little thing", and then we will start to see some progress. I am in no way implying that the world is doing nothing whatsoever to aid poor countries – we are simply not doing enough. There are a number of things that we can do. For example, small statutory deductions from the public's wages, taken by the government and given to the billions of starving humans in Africa and other areas blighted by hunger and poverty. Also, better liaison between powerful governments, such as America, Ireland and the United Kingdom, and the often corrupt African governments would help the African governments to realise that the welfare of their civilians is the most important thing. There also needs to be an increase in the number of aid workers that go out to impoverished countries to do volunteer work. In some ways, these generous people can be more effective than a donation, as they bring hope and joy to the hungry, diseased people that they help.

To conclude Mr President, I would like to say that I have great respect for you and I am certain that you will give this problem your fullest attention, by encouraging other world leaders to join you in your attempt to end the torture of billions of fellow human beings.

Yours faithfully,

Eoin Ferry

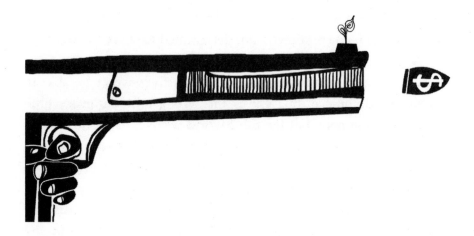

# THIRD PLACE – JUNIOR

# Barry Maguire
*Ireland, Age 14*

**Subject:** CHILD LABOUR

Dear President Obama,

I am writing to you on the topic of child labour which I believe to be a major issue facing the world today. The problem is that too many people don't know where the goods they're buying or the clothes they're wearing are coming from, where they are made, who makes them and how they are treated.

Jack is twelve-years-old and lives in the US, this morning he woke up at eight and got up out of his warm, cosy bed. He walked downstairs where his mother and father were getting breakfast ready for themselves, Jack and his six-year-old sister. On this particular morning Jack ate a bowl of Fruit Loops, though not his favourite cereal he would have to make do. As well as his cereal Jack had some pancakes, toast and a glass of orange juice. Jack wasn't very hungry on the morning in question so he left half of his cereal, his toast and the majority of his orange juice before getting ready to head off to school. Like most boys of his age, Jack isn't especially fond of school but he goes because he must.

A number of hours earlier at five in the morning a boy named Minh makes up on the streets in the slums of Hanoi, Vietnam on a bed of hard concrete that is a refuge from the broken glass that surrounds him; a smell of decomposing rubbish fills the air. Minh, like the thousands of other children living in the slums of Hanoi, is an orphan. His parents died of malaria, they could not afford the five dollars for a mosquito net. Minh is the oldest of four brothers and he sees himself responsible for all of them. It was his mother's last words: "Take care of your brothers," she said. "Take care of them". A child should not have to grow up this quickly. The brothers begin to walk through the slums, all around them they see children like them waking up and beginning to go scavenging through waste looking for anything they can sell, but unlike these children Minh and his brothers work in a factory tanning leather.

Jack got into the car followed by his sister and father, and just like every other child in the neighbourhood they drove to school each with their car half empty down the road to the school just a mile away. Neither Jack nor his sister were too pleased about going to school; neither liked it but little did they know how many other children would love to get the chance to go to school as they do.

And so they arrived at school where they played with their friends in the playground and learned about History, Maths, Geography and English. At lunchtime Jack eats a wholesome meal.

Minh and his brothers have begun their work at the leather factory. Their job is to put the leather into the great big chemical vats and to clean them of hairs. Minh climbs into the vat and begins to mix the chemicals around with his feet and stamp on the leather to get the hair off. The chemicals burn his legs and they itch but he knows he can't stop working or one of the men will hit him with one of the big rubber pipes lying on the ground. Minh has learned this the hard way – he has a number of scars up and down his back as do his brothers and the hundreds of other children that work in the factory.

While Minh works in the factory Jack is out playing with his friends as children should; he plays on the street and has fun with his friends, completely unaware as to what thousands of children

14

like him have to do to survive. While in the factory Minh and his brothers get one meal. This is why they do the work and this is why they must come back to the factory – if they don't they die. The meal isn't exactly the finest French cuisine though – it consists of one bowl of gruel. Now you may think stories like this exist only in the stories of Charles Dickens but this is the reality for *159 million* child labourers worldwide.

As Jack is settling down for bed at nine o'clock, Minh is still hard at work. He can feel the searing pain of the chemicals eating away at his skin, he must work hard, the leather is being shipped out the next day and he will be beaten if he doesn't have it ready on time. Minh thinks to himself, who would buy this stuff? This leather, if only they knew how it was made, but the reality is that few people know where their clothes were made. Do you? Do you know who made your clothes and how they were treated? The reality is that the consumer doesn't know if their clothes, or anything they buy, were made with child labour and it is very possible that the leather Minh is working, that is causing him sickness from inhaling it, will end up forming some part of Jack's ensemble, though of course he wouldn't know it.

Finally Minh and his brothers finish work and are allowed go home, but they have no home. While Jack is gone to bed over two hours, Minh is looking for a place to sleep, not sure if it is safe for him to close his eyes if he does find somewhere for fear he will be attacked.

And so I ask you president Obama to stop child labour and punish severely all those companies found to be using child labour, stopping children from growing up and getting an education, for as I'm sure you're well aware many American companies have been found to be using child labour and yet they proceed to do so. Tell the people what is going on. Would you buy a pair of shoes made from the leather Minh made? Not if you knew how he was treated and about his life.

# SHORTLIST – JUNIOR

## Ciarán McFarland
*Northern Ireland, Age 15*

**Subject: CHILD LABOUR**

Dear President Obama,

I would like to congratulate you on your inauguration into the US Presidency and on your incredible achievement of being the first African-American President of the USA.

I am writing to you about the biggest problem in our planet, namely of world hunger. I am going to show you how horrific, appalling and heart-breaking the lives of some of these people's lives are, I hope that you will see that world hunger needs to end or be dramatically reduced soon.

I wish to begin with some eye opening facts to illustrate how bad the situation is:

In 2008 the number of undernourished people in the world rose to 963 million people. This is higher than the population of the USA, Canada and the European Union put together.

Hunger and malnutrition are the number one health risk in the world, greater than AIDS, malaria and tuberculosis combined.

Today 25,000 people will die from hunger. We have heard in commercials in the media that a child dies every three seconds. But just counting children is being ignorant. A person dies every second of hunger. So look at your clock. Every time the little, thin delicate hand twitches, ever so slightly, a person has died of hunger. A family have lost someone close to them. This needs to stop.

In my opinion this is unacceptable. In the Western World we don't appreciate how lucky we are. Every day we can eat whenever we want. Every day we are guaranteed to have meals placed in front of us. We eat at least three times a day not to mention our sneaky trips to the refrigerator for a snack between meals.

Yet we dare use the phrase "I'm starving" or "I'm hungry". I see this as being incredibly ignorant as we don't have an idea of what the word means. There are poor, weak and innocent little children out there who go for days and days without anything to eat. Perhaps we should remember that a little snack that we consider small, meaningless and insignificant that it would not make a difference think to yourself that this would be all a child in India or Africa would eat for three to four days.

Some people ask, "Who is to blame for World Hunger?" or "Why is this happening?" Two of the major factors explaining this are:

1 – Greedy, selfish, ignorant corporate owners of food companies. At the minute these multibillionaire tycoons are worrying about the "Credit Crunch". They are increasing their prices of food dramatically, not so they can survive, but so they can maintain their extravagant lifestyles and can still buy their exclusive yachts, private jets and unnecessarily large mansions. They don't need all this money they are gaining, yet they are making it impossible for the people in poverty in undeveloped countries to buy food at all. Prices have gone up so much that people can't even afford the necessities they need to survive. So these men are putting people's lives in jeopardy just so they can live in more comfort. I see this as completely selfish, narrow-minded and self-indulgent. I do not know how these men can live with themselves knowing what effect their selfishness is having on others.

2 – Another major aspect of the problem of world hunger is the fact that governments are wasting millions of dollars on things that are completely unnecessary. We see countries paying billions on Olympic Games. Billions on high pay for their staff, while people in

less developed countries can't buy enough food to survive. I'll give you a startling fact: The world spends over 1,000 billion dollars on military, while a 40 billion dollar increase in funds could feed, clothe and educate the entire world. Now that is unacceptable. Maybe every country needs defence. But just think a few less planes or tanks, less guns or less bombs, could end world hunger completely. Does the USA or Iran need nuclear weapons? Is having a more impressive military more important than saving the lives of millions of people? Surely a slight decrease in production of arms is one way of releasing funds for food programmes in undeveloped countries.

Most depressingly of all, Mr President, is the fact that the situation is getting worse. The number of hungry people in the world increased by 80 million from 1990 to 2007. In 2007 to 2008 it went up 40 million. With all the advances in technology and the increase of awareness of world hunger surely we should be improving the situation? Yet the opposite is happening as people are getting scared about the credit crunch and are forgetting that we might not be able to buy our luxuries during this time, people don't have enough money to survive. People are being less generous to charities and the effects of this are shown in the figures I have shown you.

The thing that angers and annoys me most about the situation of world hunger is that there is enough food in the world to feed everyone. The world produces about enough food to keep 12 billion people healthy – more than twice the world's population. The total food surplus of the United States could feed every empty stomach in Africa. France's leftovers could feed the hungry in the Democratic Republic of Congo. Italy's leftovers could feed Ethiopia's undernourished.

So where is all this food going? People are eating far more than their recommended calorie intake. People are wasting food by not eating it and disposing of it in waste bins. I think we should be more efficient with our food. We should eat the right amount of food and not waste as much food. If we do these things we could decrease the problem of world hunger greatly as well as improving our health and reducing levels of obesity.

Also, I think all developed countries should take part in the United Nation's attempt to end world hunger by giving 0.7% of the country's national income to international aid. Twenty-two countries have agreed to donate this money but only five countries have met the goal, with others lagging, including your own country. Now, I need to ask why is it that the richest nation in the entire world can't donate a tiny percentage of its income to help people who are leading bleak, hungry and joyless lives? Surely this is more important than leisure or other unnecessary luxuries. Is it more important to make sure your people can enjoy themselves in a million different ways or to save millions of lives? It's your decision.

In conclusion, this letter has one simple message. We can end world hunger, if we each take a step in the right direction and take a tiny piece of luxury from our lives. It's up to every individual to help this happen. You as the president of the world's wealthiest and most powerful economy can save millions of lives. The world needs you to help change many people's lives and I hope I have encouraged you to help end world hunger.

Ciarán McFarland

# SHORTLIST – JUNIOR

## Kyro Iskander

*Unites States, Age 14*

**Subject: WORLD HUNGER**

Dear Mr. President Barack Obama,

Every day I pray for you and your family. I hear my parents talk about it being a very challenging time to lead our nation and I know so much is expected from you, maybe more than any other president of our time. As I watched your victory and celebration I saw young/old laugh and cry. You brought the promise of hope and opportunity to a new day that many Americans thought would never come. It must be hard to sleep at night thinking of all the tasks you have ahead. I imagine it to be like playing a basketball game with the world watching every day and being expected to make every shot. I am sure you feel you can't afford to have a bad game because so many people's lives depend on you to get it right. Don't worry! I know you believe in God, and will depend on him for wisdom and strength.

Today, I write to you in this same spirit of hope and wisdom to direct some of your focus on behalf of the "one in eight children under 12" in the US who goes to bed hungry every night in the "world's wealthiest nation". I am the cry of the "man or child who every 3.6 seconds dies of hunger in the world", but can't speak for themselves. As we ask for our "Daily Bread" we must be able to generously share it. This is our commitment of "yes we can"; right the wrong of people dying of poverty in a world that has plenty.

Allowing starvation to exist around the world is shameful. When considering that according to the United Nations, studies show that "The world already produces more than enough to feed everyone on the planet and has the capacity to produce even more." Yet still 860 million people go hungry on any given day. Many people have lots of extra food and waste it, while the poor can't count on a loaf of bread to quiet the pain of an empty stomach or the agony of a hungry malnourished child. Hunger and malnutrition kill more people every year than Aids, malaria and TB combined.

Hunger causes people to starve to death and affects them negatively in other ways. Poor health leads to low energy, and disables the mind. A vicious cycle is created as hunger can cause more poverty by reducing a person's ability to work and learn. How would you feel if you didn't eat for days, leaving you delirious and impairing your mental status? What if you went hungry just because of where you were born? What is the chance of these kids dreaming of becoming president, instead of when and if they will get their next meal? Every year 15 million children die of hunger. This hurts us all because these children don't even get a chance to live life or affect the world. A quote that was written by an unknown person, "Where you live should not determine whether you live … It's not charity it's justice." The kids in poor places such as Africa die just because they were born there. They have no choices or options to change their life. This is terrible because I'm sure one of these fifteen million children could positively change or impact our world.

To satisfy the world's sanitation and food requirements it would only cost thirteen billion dollars. That is what the people of the US and the European Union spend on perfume each year. I think it's pathetic that we sacrifice a life instead of a lifestyle. I find it disheartening we only donate .16% of our income and the United Nations agree to pay .7% of the countries' income. It is bewildering to me that we choose destruction over saving lives.

The price of one missile could feed lunch to a school full of starving kids for five years!

Most of the food is produced in economically more developed countries such as the US. The countries in need of food cannot afford the high prices the farmers charge. To solve this we need to encourage the national government and state departments to subsidise the purchase of food by less economically developed countries. These poor countries also owe 376 billion dollars in debt. The repayments take a large part of each country's income, leaving little left to help solve their hunger issues. The US could help by negotiating on behalf of these nations to convince government officials to cancel world debt.

Lack of education is another huge problem. A Chinese poet wrote:

> *If you are thinking one year ahead, sow a seed.*
> *If you are thinking ten years ahead, plant a tree.*
> *If you are thinking one hundred years ahead, educate the*
>    *people.*
> *By sowing a seed once, you will harvest once.*
> *By planting a tree, you will harvest tenfold.*
> *By educating the people you will harvest one hundred fold.*

Or a more common quote.

> *Give a man a fish and he will eat a meal.*
> *Teach a man to fish and he will eat for a lifetime.*

Education was mentioned in both quotes because education is the key to survival. As a result we need to educate the people, so we can provide them with a permanent solution to hunger.

There is nothing we can't do as a nation; our history tells the story before and after 9-11. To heal we must help others to heal. "If one member suffers all the members suffer with it" (1 Corithians 12:26). "To those who have bread, may they give gen-

22

erously, hungering for justice" (Rev. Garth Hanson). I urge you Mr President to take up this cause and take decisive action to end world hunger leading our nation to be remembered for feeding our brothers.

Sincerely,

Kyro I.

# SHORTLIST – JUNIOR

# Karl Milne
## *Ireland, Age 15*

### Subject: WORLD HUNGER

Dear President Obama,
Firstly I would sincerely like to congratulate you on behalf of my country on winning the election. I genuinely hope that you can bring change to the USA, and not just to America but to her fellow continents across the globe.

I have paid a substantial amount of attention listening to your speeches in which you talk about the audacity of hope, the pursuit of happiness and worldwide equality. I must commend you for the faith you have given your supporters, including those who have little faith to start with. I am going to talk to you about the paramount issue of worldwide hunger, which I believe is crippling the planet's ever-fluctuating population as well as hampering any improvement in less developed countries.

As I am sure you know already, one out of six people in the world suffer from inexorable poverty and hunger on a day-to-day basis. It is in countries like Ethiopia, Zambia and Uganda that starvation is most prevalent. The statistics illustrate this all too clearly; in countries like Mali for every 1,000 infants born, 140 perish due to severe hunger.

Another surprising figure: it is estimated that 40,000 children suffer from malnutrition daily. Similarly, these regions are all victims of variable hindrances that deprive their people of education, health services and development schemes. These obstructions range from a spectrum of causes such as international debt, population control and unfair trading patterns. While all of these difficulties have damaging effects on Third World countries, they appear to originate from the same source: the First World.

Countries that have high GNPs and whose people enjoy a decent standard of living have a widely acknowledged history of imposing unfair conditions on indigent regions. For instance, in the eighteenth century when the British Empire was at its zenith it colonised a great number of lands in Africa for plantations. Since those times these empires have collapsed and the plantations have ended, yet the First World still seems to have leverage on Least Developed Countries (LDCs). Allow me to verify this statement with an example. Brazil has one of the world's primary coffee bean exports. One of its main trading-partners is the US, which purchases their coffee beans at a low pay rate. The statistics speak for themselves: 82% of the profits earned by the coffee industry go to the First World, whereas only 18% is given to the growers in Underdeveloped Countries. This is on account of two factors: the First World's unfair price settings with the poorer continents, and that most of the money made from coffee comes from coffee manufacturing. Having learned this, Brazil initially planned to establish its own processing industry. Then the United States threatened to cut aid with Brazil, and consequentially any aspirations to form an indigent coffee-making industry were abandoned. Furthermore, this validates the unfair trading patterns between the rich and poor continents.

But how does this impact on human health? Simple: it results in countries having a lower GNP, and therefore an exiguous standard of living. This is illustrated clearly on the National Cycle of Poverty. Low income leads to low saving, which ultimately results in low productivity. Since there is low involvement in agriculture, there is paucity of food supply, and in turn a starving population. Having understood this, we can be confident that world hunger is a major issue in our global development, and that the First World has a significant part to play in it. But just as it can have negative effects, it can be used to facilitate improvement in Less Developed Countries. But how?

First World countries, namely the UK and US, could be more charitable with their wealth. Bilateral aid programmes can be a major asset to these economically poor countries, as long as they are not made conditional by governments. For decades the United States have been donating yearly contributions that, though substantially proportioned, either come tied with conditions or demand some form of recompense. This is hardly the aid LDCs require, especially those such as Ethiopia and Lesotho where the death rate is surpassing the birth rate. If the Developed World is to offer any form of aid it should be purely altruistic and without reciprocal intentions. This is unfortunately not the case for most bilateral aid programmes, and serves as a major obviator that lessens the quasi "generous aid" that we rich countries are supplying. But this can be prevented by more development aid programmes and less direct contributions.

There has been a range of development programmes organised by non-governmental organisations that specialise in promoting primary activities. This includes fishing, forestry and mining, or essentially teaching countries how to provide for themselves without direct interference from the First World. These procedures have had a history of widely acknowledged success. If implemented even further, and perhaps invested in more so than dumping direct bilateral onto Undeveloped Countries, their economies would rise out of independent understanding of how to provide for themselves. Essentially, this is what I am trying to state: "Give a man a fish and he will eat for a day. Teach a man how to fish and he will eat for a lifetime." Mr. President, I for one along with many others think it is the time to do the latter, before things continue to worsen in our crippling world. By battling debt, unfair trade and combating widespread hunger through prudence instead of pretentious grace we can help preserve many countries.

In conclusion, I hope you have paid heed to what I have had to say on the controversial matter of worldwide hunger. I trust in your astute eye for worldwide equality to bring issues like world hunger to an end, and also to improve the one billion lives who are daily victims of unyielding starvation and malnutrition.

Yours faithfully,

Karl Milne

# SHORTLIST – JUNIOR

# Leanne Murray

## *Ireland, Age 14*

**Subject: WORLD HUNGER**

Dear President Obama,

First of all, I would like to congratulate you on becoming the 44th President of the United States of America. I thought your inauguration speech was very inspiring. The eyes of the whole world will be upon you, to see if you will carry out your promises that you made in your campaign. I hope you will try and solve some of the problems that America and indeed the world faces.

One of the biggest issues the world faces is global hunger. I was particularly touched by a certain part of your inauguration speech, "to the people of poor nations we pledge to work alongside you to make your farms flourish, and let clean water flow, to nourish starved bodies and feed hungry minds". How do you intend for America to help other countries, when America is in serious debt? Now that we are in a recession, people aren't going to make as many donations.

Every 3.6 seconds someone dies of hunger; there are 923 million people across the world starving. As your ancestors would have experienced, places like Africa and Asia are some of the poorest nations in the world. Why is it that when there was plenty of wealth in the world [disposable income] for the last ten to fifteen years, the problems of hunger were not solved? What chance is there now to solve these same problems, now that the whole world is in recession? Where is the money going to come from? Every country has to contribute to solve this problem.

Mr. President, I read a very disturbing fact that one out of every eight children under the age of 12 in the United States goes to bed hungry every night. This is an appalling statistic, seeing as the United States of America is [supposed to be] one of the richest nations of the world. The buck stops here, it's time to take action against these problems. Firstly America has to get to grips with their own poverty and hunger problems, which go hand in hand. As you have said in your speech, "to nourish starved bodies and feed hungry minds", how are these problems going to be solved? How does your government intend to tackle these problems?

One of the biggest contributory factors of global hunger is climate change, because countries along the equator are getting too hot to grow crops, to provide food for the people of these countries. What these countries need are volunteers to help provide water by digging wells. With this water people can grow crops to feed their families. These people will be healthier due to the clean water. The people of these countries also need an education and to achieve this, they need voluntary teachers – but to do all this they need money. Where is the money going to come from?

Is the answer to all these problems another Live Aid, as happened in 1985? As you are the most high profile world leader, the rest of the world looks up to you, to lead by example and not leave it to the musicians of the world to raise money. I think I have come up with a great solution: why not bring into law a once off tax on mega rich people, such as people from the music industry, like singers [agents}, bands, record companies. People from the film industry, like actors-actresses, directors, and sports stars, such as soccer players, tennis players etc... I think a tax of 10 percent of their earnings would be fair. For example, Madonna earned $120 MILLION last year alone. This amount of money ($12 million) is impossible to spend in an average person's lifetime. This amount of money is just a drop in the ocean for such celebrities, but this amount of money would make an enormous difference to countries in the developing world.

To conclude, the problem of global hunger will not go away on its own. It's time to take action. I know you have a very busy schedule at the moment but I would be very grateful if you took the time to respond to some of the issues I have raised in my letter. The whole world is watching you, with anticipation, to see if all the promises you have vowed to make during your presidency will come into fruition. I hope you have enjoyed my letter.

Yours Sincerely,

Leanne Murray

# SHORTLIST – JUNIOR

# Sarah Crompton
## *United Kingdom, Age 13*

### Subject: CLIMATE CHANGE

Dear President Obama,

Our earth is fighting back for the harm we have caused her. We have abused her, milked her shamelessly for her resources, cut down her forests for cheap paper, wood and land, polluted her oceans, and burned oil and coal and gas, poisoning the life-giving air that she gave as a gift to every living thing.

So she is rebelling, with floods, drought, tsunamis, hurricanes, typhoons, storms and earthquakes.

A tooth for a tooth, an eye for an eye. .

But in this cruel game of revenge, anybody's tooth will do, anybody's eye.

In a fair world, a man is not imprisoned for his neighbour's crime, so why is it that the poorest and most vulnerable people in our world are being punished for the reckless behaviour of their more fortunate, more foolish counterparts?

The poorest people in the world will be the hardest hit by the effects of climate change, and there is very little that they can do to help themselves.

It is all of the developed countries that have caused this problem, and it is the developed countries that must solve it.

Sub-Saharan Africa is responsible for less than three per cent of the world's greenhouse gas emissions, yet it would be hit very badly by climate change.

Over half of the African population live in rural areas and rely on the local environment for growing food, and with already unreliable rainfall, rising temperatures and drought would have a devastating effect on crops.

Unbearable thirst.

Unbearable hunger.

Unbearable suffering, and then, finally, the … relief of death.

Changes in temperature and rainfall would also trigger malaria outbreaks because of faster breeding in mosquitoes.

Malaria already kills between 675,000 and 1,000,000 children in sub-Saharan Africa every year. About 1,000,000 mothers lose a child to malaria, every single year.

Every 365 days, one million mothers have their hearts ripped out. They see their children's eyes, filled with fear and pain as they are seized by the fever, the shivering, the vomiting, the anaemia.

They see their children shook by terrifying convulsions, then finally slip into a malaria coma, a sleep from which they will never wake.

One million.

Do we want to make that number bigger?

Do we want *our* children, the next generation, to solve this problem, and then look back at us with disgust because we let things spiral so hopelessly out of control? Because we mindlessly and unconcernedly let it happen, thinking that it couldn't possibly be *our* fault, burying our heads in the sand?

Africa is not the only continent that is going to be shattered because of the developed world's irresponsible and selfish deeds.

Asia, especially heavily populated coastal areas in the mega delta regions in the South, East and South-East. will be at an incredible risk due to increased flooding from the sea and rivers.

People's houses, swallowed by dark, murky water, their few precious belongings ruined, destroyed.

These are people just like us.

They are less fortunate versions of ourselves.

It is also predicted that river flow will decrease, meaning that freshwater availability would decline dramatically, affecting more than half a billion people by 2050.

Half a billion. A number so large, so incomprehensible.

That many people, suffering.

Half a billion people without one basic requirement for life – water.

No water to drink, wash with, cook with, water their crops, feed their animals.

Half a billion. Unimaginable. But, in about 40 years' time, if we don't do anything, it will become a painful reality.

Why do we, humans, always have to destroy the beautiful environment that Mother Nature gave us?

We provide the market for the destruction of the beautiful rainforests of South America.

True, it is not directly our fault. *We* do not cut down the trees, or burn them to make space for cattle ranches.

But we provide a market for these things, we are ready made buyers.

The developed world is eager to purchase cheap timber, cheap paper, and corned beef from cattle ranches in Brazil.

In this way, South America is contributing to climate change, because in cutting down the world's largest rainforest, the Amazon, the lungs of the earth are being destroyed, a place where animals and plants and indigenous peoples live in harmony.

We could learn so much from this place, yet it is chopped down for material gain.

And they are also vital if we are to tackle climate change – the average tree "breathes in" about one tonne of $CO_2$ over 100 years.

So why is it that 1.5 acres of rainforest is lost every second of every day?

Why is this allowed to happen?

Of course, South America is also greatly affected by climate change.

By 2050, the population in South America will be about 50% larger than it was in 2000, and the frequency of weather extremes and natural disasters will increase.

The terror of South America, the El Niño phenomenon, which contributes greatly to the occurrence of natural disasters such as floods and droughts, looks set to worsen.

El Niño occurs when the sea surface temperature rises to over 0.5 degrees across the central tropical Pacific Ocean.

It brings warm wet summers along Peru, Ecuador, Brazil and Argentina, often causing major flooding.

Colombia, the Amazon River Basin and Central America get drier and hotter weather which leads to water shortages and drought.

El Niño also considerably damages fishing in many parts of South America because it reduces the nutrients in the water that sustain fish populations, which is disastrous as the fish are a main source of food for a lot of people.

Hunger, again.

What can we, the developed countries, do?

It's complicated, yes, but aren't we always told that humans are the most intelligent species on this earth?

We'd better start behaving like it.

We'd better solve this problem, together, and save the people that we have put in danger.

# SHORTLIST – JUNIOR

## Stephanie McGrath

*Ireland, Age 13*

**Subject:** WORLD HUNGER

Dear President Obama,

I live in a beautiful world, a world of freshly scented air, a world of fresh, flowing water. A world of so many beautiful sights, sounds, textures and flavours. Strong colours, soft pastels and even the black night sky is breathtaking. There is a population of about 6.78 billion on Planet Earth. All of us waking up underneath the same sky, standing above the same layers of crust, magma and core. All of our days lit by the same sun, all of us waking up to Planet Earth. Although some don't wake up to the same world. One in twelve people woke today to a different world from you and me, born into a different world, a different world, Mr. Obama.

Hunger is a term which has three meanings. The uneasy or painful sensation caused by want of food craving appetite; the exhausted condition caused by want of food; the want or scarcity of food in a country, a strong desire or craving. Yet this is just the technical meaning. I'm sure we can't imagine how it feels to be a sufferer of world hunger. I'm sure we'll never know how it feels to be born hungry, to live hungry and to die hungry. Every 3.6 seconds someone dies of hunger, someone with needs and rights. Family and friends, yet their needs are not met, their rights are not taken into account and most of the people they know are also dying from hunger.

With so much pain, with so much death and so much hunger, it's hard to believe there's such a simple cure. Food. Food is a basic human right, yet two-thirds of the world are under-fed or starving. To satisfy the world's sanitation and food requirements would cost only $13 billion. What the people of the United States and the European Union spend on perfume each year. I am honestly frightened by that statistic. There are so many ways we can prevent world hunger, Mr. Obama, simple, easy ways to stop the painful suffering of starvation.

Distribution is a large problem. The amount of grain produced in the world today could provide each person on the planet with the equivalent of two loaves of bread per day. Our current food production could feed 7 billion people. That's more than the population of earth. It is the distribution of this food that is the problem. Most of our food is produced in more developed countries, which leaves the countries in need of food unable to afford the high prices these farmers charge. This can be solved by governments giving financial support to the purchase of food by less economically developed countries.

In the words of John Lennon, give peace a chance. Not only would this make the world a much better place, it would aid in preventing world hunger. War diverts funds from starving people to weapons and the war process. Peace negotiations help to allow aid in and the country to focus its time onto solving their hunger problems. If the War in Iraq was stopped for four days, the money that would've been used would fund the population of earth to be educated for one year. Of course, education plays a huge part of preventing world hunger.

In 500 BC, an anonymous Chinese poet wrote:

*If you are thinking a year ahead, sow seed*

*If you are thinking ten years ahead, plant a tree*

*If you are thinking one hundred years ahead, educate the*
*    people*

*By sowing a see once, you will harvest once*

*By planting a tree, you will harvest tenfold*

*By educating the people, you will harvest one hundredfold*

Education allows people to focus their energy on projects. Once you have a proper education, you can receive a job, then a wage and then food. Education not only helps hunger, it helps the economy and the country's future.

You've inspired so many hearts all over the globe. I know you have the power to inspire people to stop world hunger. President Barack Obama, I beg you please. Help stop the hunger, help change the lives of starving people, help make the Third World, the Developed World, the world itself, into one world, a world of freshly scented air and fresh, flowing water, into one hunger-free world.

A beautiful world.

# SHORTLIST JUNIOR

# Maria McWalter
*Ireland, Age 15*

### Subject: CHILD LABOUR

Dear President Obama,

I would firstly like to congratulate you on your successful presidential campaign. I'm honoured that you've taken time out of your busy schedule to read my letter. President Obama, "Injustice anywhere is a threat to justice everywhere". Therefore, I'm writing to you on behalf of 250 million children across the world. I believe that child labour is unnecessary in today's society. It is unnecessary because I believe it is caused solely by corruption, greed and inaction. There's no denying that child labourers are suffering. I hope that you can take my views on this serious issue into account. So, you will have a new perspective on how to end this suffering.

From the diamond mines of Botswana to the coffee plantations of Brazil, child labour is clearly a widespread problem in the Third World. A typical day for a child labourer begins before dawn. Most children go to work on an empty stomach. They face a long day which may last for up to sixteen hours and they are unlikely to receive any breaks. Factory owners are simply too poor to provide child workers with decent working conditions. Sweat factories in poor countries are poorly ventilated and children are prone to fainting in these stifling conditions. Worryingly, over 30,000 children die in work-related accidents each year. Many more suffer from chronic respiratory illnesses caused by dust and exposure to asbestos. Every one of the 250 million child labourers in our world has made a sacrifice. They have sacrificed their education by working seventy hours per week. They have sacrificed their safety by working with sharp and faulty machinery. Do they really need to sacrifice their dreams, their futures or even their lives just so they can earn a pitiful wage? We need to stop this injustice now before it's too late. Millions of children will never learn to read or write and in years to come they will be unable to obtain any qualifications. However, if children are given the opportunity to attend school then they will face a brighter future. In addition, a child dies every three seconds in the Third World due to starvation – we do not have time. Money is immaterial, these kid's lives are what matter.

Child labourers sacrifice everything just so their family can improve their livelihood. But $0.20 an hour is not enough for these children, and that's if they get paid which they rarely do. Adults' wages are just as low. To end child labour once and for all, it is vital that you, President Obama, work towards increasing adults' wages. By increasing their wages, it will become unnecessary for children as young as five to enter the workplace. You have previously insisted that children are the most valuable resource in society. So, I plead with you President Obama, please invest in these children's futures by increasing wages in the Third World immediately. Who knows, a child currently working in a sweat factory could one day become a famous doctor or lawyer. Sadly, many young people in the Third World are forced into the world of drugs. Over 40% of Botswana's workforce is in the drugs industry.

In addition, I believe that factory owners in countries such as India should accept necessary safety legislation for their workers. Due to bad conditions in sweat factories, averages of 30,000 children die each year in the Third World. Therefore, it is vital that you continue to put pressure on world leaders to enforce this life-saving procedure. For example, by making fire exits compulsory in all workplaces and by making sure regular breaks are allocated. I believe that you cannot put a price on these children's safety.

What kills 21 million people each year? Shockingly, it's Third World debt. That's more than four times the population of Ireland, dying as a result of debt every year. African countries spend over $40 million each year servicing its debt to developed countries. Corrupt African Governments squandered the money they borrowed from the Developed World. Consequently, African people have paid a steep price for this debt. They are struggling to repay the money they never spent. I know that child labour will be difficult and costly for Developed Nations to solve. But as I said, money is immaterial – these kid's lives are what matter. That's why Third World debt should be cancelled so child labour can be stopped.

Finally, I believe that growers in developing countries should receive a fair price for their produce. It is well-documented that growers of coffee in Brazil only receive 8% of the money got from coffee sales. This is due to taxes and tariffs that have been charged by wealthy multinational companies. President Obama, our world leaders need to end this selfishness because poor countries will never be self-sufficient if they continue to be swindled by "fat cats".

It's for these reasons that I feel strongly about ending child labour. I believe that children in the Third World need to be given a voice so their case can be heard and I believe they should receive the human rights that they're entitled to. I hope I have given you a clear perspective on this issue. To reiterate on my opening statement, "Injustice anywhere is a threat to justice everywhere". This was an important principle for one inspirational man. This man had one dream, one voice and one vision. He overcame oppression to give millions of people a voice who had been previously ignored. This man was Doctor Martin Luther King and his pursuit for peace and justice changed the world forever. It shows us that an inspirational leader can overcome any obstacle no matter how difficult. So, as the world embraces you as a new hopeful leader, I plead with you, President Obama, to give these children a voice. So, together this world can work together for a brighter and peaceful future.

Yours truly,

On behalf of the 250 million child labourers.

# SHORTLIST JUNIOR

# Chris Kane
*Ireland, Age 15*

### Subject: CHILD LABOUR

Dear President Obama,

First of all may I congratulate you upon winning the election and I wish you the best of luck in the running of the United States of America. I am writing to you to talk to you about the pressing issue of climate change. America did not sign the Kyoto protocol as America said it would have brought US industry to a halt. This maybe be so, but let me plant some images into your head about what could happen if nothing is done about climate change.

The many polar bears in Alaska will no longer survive, the many picturesque landscapes and majestic, rare and wonderful animals of the Rockies and Yellowstone will no longer exist. When the great, majestic and mighty Niagara Falls dries up due to the increase in temperature. Think even of your own Hawaii, now longer containing the amazing and beautiful landscapes and wildlife. The many beautiful and unique landscapes of Ireland would be no more.

With sea levels due to rise by up to 88 centimetres by 2100, what will happen to the people of New Orleans, Galveston and many of the other hurricane-torn cities knocking on America's door? What will happen if tornados and flash floods become more frequent? What will happen when heavy snow hits the north western states and outside help gaining entry is impossible?

Doomsday scenarios are what I have just described and all because America wouldn't think about the melting ice caps and all grow more and more likely every second America sits in limbo as it fears the loss of jobs and industry. America, wake up and smell the roses. Climate change is a serious issue.

Even in these recessionary times, when everybody is worried about their job and lifestyle, nobody is talking as much about the environment. The issue of climate change could have as much an effect on our lifestyles as this recession. I am aware that the main issue coming into your office is the recession but please spare a thought for the environment as it could cause as much hardship as this recession.

Mr. President I will now propose a few simple ideas to help to get America on track. A congestion charge in major towns and cities. The fees I propose are nothing extreme as in these times many people aren't very willing to part with much of their money. At $3.00 for residents of the town or city, $5.00 for other vehicles and $8.00 dollars for lorries and $6.00 or more axle trucks, these figures don't break the bank.

This is for every two days driving in the town or city. I have done some calculations and if 10 million of New York's 18.8 million residents drove in the city for two days, total revenue raised would be $30 million. Over time this additional revenue could go back into public transport projects in the city with revenue collected and into projects which keep the city's public services.

Thank you Mr. President for your time and I hope I have encouraged you to start to try and reduce America's $CO_2$ emissions as you as well as I hope that the day will never come when your beloved Honolulu becomes as baron as the Sahara, as lifeless as the Arctic and as dead as Death Valley.

Yours Sincerely,

Chris Kane

# PASSAGES, EXTRACTS, QUOTES – JUNIOR CATEGORY

## Alex Crean

*Ireland, Age 14*

**Subject:** CHILD LABOUR

Watching the news lately has been tough as it is all doom and gloom but I am writing to you about a far bigger problem than we experience most days. This monstrosity I am talking about is child labour. Even though it doesn't receive the news time it deserves or even gets talked about as a major global problem it invariably affects all of us in some way. How many of our houses are cluttered with junk made by poor starving children working for pennies in Pakistan? It is perhaps a question most of us would prefer not to answer. The statistics and figures are there. All we need now is for people to say no

The real cause of this problem though is the employers who think it's all right to make a little extra profit. No harm, it's only a child's life! They can pay as little as they want because it's only starving families that suffer and their working conditions can be as bad as they want because who cares what the poor seven-year-old is complaining about? Companies who profit from child labour should be immediately boycotted by all first world countries and who, Mr. President, would better to lead the way than you. As the leader of one of the most if not the most powerful countries in the world the onus is on you to make a difference and we all know that if you put a step in the right direction many others will follow.

According to the World Watch Institute, the annual expenditure on perfume is $15 billion while achieving universal literacy would only need an annual investment of $5 billion. This shows that if anyone did just their little bit then we can let these children learn and break the cycle that has been restraining them. Education is the key to ending the exploitation of children.

All around the world people are now opening their eyes and seeing what problems we have. Child labour is not the only problem facing us today, far from it, and it would be inconsiderate on my part to ask you to totally focus on this.

I can only hope that you will try, as you are the man who can change it all from your position of power. In this day and age we see revolutions almost every year. From technological, like the age of the internet, to social, like your own presidency, it is a time for change. Let's push forward for one more major revolution and do what might have seemed impossible ten years ago and to many what still seems impossible today.

Let's end child labour, everyone, together.

# Eibhlín Lonergan

*Ireland, Age 14*

## Subject: WORLD HUNGER

I hope you will not consider me presumptuous to write this letter to you. I am a 14-year-old Irish schoolgirl, who takes an interest in political and international affairs. Firstly I wish to offer you my heartiest congratulations on your inauguration, and to say that your oratory and sincerity have left a lasting impression on the whole world. We all feel safer and more secure with you at the helm in the most powerful nation in the world.

I know that you intend to inject a huge amount of dollars into the American economy to restore it to a healthy condition. In your generosity and compassion for the less fortunate, I am sure you will see your way to spare a very small fraction of this huge financial infection for the cholera-ridden sick of Zimbabwe, or for some other poverty-stricken country. Then, as the son of an African father, you can proudly say, "I did not forget my place of origin".

I could not finish without mentioning your Irish roots and the great celebrations which the people of Moneygall had on your inauguration day. This is a small, rural village in the centre of Ireland – perhaps like the village in which your grandmother lives. It was from this village your maternal ancestors emigrated to America, fleeing from famine and fever during the Irish Famine. As you can see, neither of us are very far removed from the great tragedies which we witness in the Third World today. Perhaps one day you will pay a visit to your ancestral home, just as John F. Kennedy did fifty years ago.

I wish you, Mrs. Obama, Malia and Sasha a pleasant, successful and peaceful period in your new home. As a young teenager I can appreciate how a change of home, and particularly a change of school, can be an ordeal. But by the calm demeanour and dignity which those two young ladies displayed on inauguration day, I am certain that they can master any situation. We all eagerly await a glimpse of that famous puppy, and I am sure your choice will be most appropriate.

May God be your companion on the arduous journey, which lies ahead of you, and may the world be a much better place due to your efforts. May you succeed in bringing dignity and equality to all, as you have set out to do.

God bless America.

# Martyn Black

*Scotland, Age 15*

## Subject: CLIMATE CHANGE

Firstly I would like to congratulate you on winning the recent election and, being Scottish, it would be nice to have a president like you here in Britain.

There are many things I would like to discuss with you, but the one thing I am going to write about is climate change and global warming. You know yourself that your country is one of the worst for polluting the world – 25% of the world's carbon dioxide emission is from the US and only 4% of your country populates the world. So from my point of view the world is in your hands. The fact that oil is to reach its peak by 2020 means there will be a big loss of jobs. By trying to find new sources of energy you should use this to your advantage by creating thousands of job opportunities.

Remember back in 2005 when New Orleans was struck by hurricane Katrina ...

Well that weather could become a very regular sight if we don't become more eco-friendly. This hurricane devastated many people's lives and thousands of people are still recovering. Maybe if we had thought about our world before we drove our hummers round the corner to work instead of walking, these people might not have had to go through their troubles. I would definitely consider telling people to walk more or cycle rather than driving there cars now because if they don't, it will be a shock to them when the worlds oil supply runs out which won't be a long wait.

# Brose Shanna

*Australia, Age 15*

## Subject: CHILD LABOUR

Poverty isn't right, and it isn't fair these children rarely get the honour of going to school and if they do, they never stay long; these children die never knowing the luxury of having a full stomach. As we worry about how we're going to afford that new car, that new gizmo that will make our lives so much easier, they worry about how they are going to afford that next meal that will have to sustain them for however long it takes them to raise the money for new food. These children are barely even four when they begin to work, these children have a very low rate of living over the age of five, why are we letting this continue?

I'll tell you why: because it is easier to turn a blind eye, pretend there's only sunshine and rainbows because we don't want to admit that there really is pain and suffering in the world. We must look at the suffering in this world, we have to stop worrying about the menial little things that plague our day to day lives and think about these children who may never even grow up. If we let this go on any longer then we are truly psychopathic, because to stare into the eyes of a child suffering from malnutrition, a child that is on their deathbed, and do nothing knowing full well that we have the resources to help, then, quite frankly, we needn't worry about going to hell because we have already reached the fiery gates and gone well beyond them.

Signed with love and hope

# Sean Crowley

*Ireland, Age 14*

## Subject: CLIMATE CHANGE

Congratulations on winning the election and on becoming the first African American President of the United States of America. My name is Sean Crowley and I am a 14-year-old citizen of Ireland of average intellect and achievements but even I can see that you are faced with many challenges. I implore you not to forget one of these among the many others, one that is not only felt in America but the world over. I'm talking about global warming and climate change, especially in the third world.

Your current policy on climate change claims it will have stopped 80 per cent of emissions by 2050. Mr. Obama, I'm sorry to tell you this, but this is far too little too late. It is estimated, by some of the best scientists in the world, that by 2050, no less than one billion people will be forced from their homes by the rise in oceans due to climate change. This is over three times the population of the United States. It is a fact that on average, every person in the United State produces 24 tonnes of carbon every year. Every starving, struggling person in the third world doesn't produce one, and yet they are the ones who will feel the real force of the floods, droughts, heat-waves. Your country, the country you are in charge of, has a responsibility for this.

For a man who speaks so much of justice, equality, rights and turning a new page, tell me where is the justice in one person creating 24 times the problem but another taking more than 24 times the consequences.

I ask you, for all the desperate people I have written of, do what you can. I have faith that through your own conscience you will find what you need to do this. I am just a boy asking a great leader to do what is right. I hope he will listen.

Yes you can...

---

# Craig Hendry
## *United Kingdom, Age 12*

### Subject: CHILD LABOUR

---

I feel strongly about this issue, even more so after viewing a BBC Three (British Broadcasting Corporation) program – "Blood, sweat and t-shirts". In this, six teenagers who were incredibly materialistic travelled to India to work in sweat shops and cotton fields. They started out in the "upper" class section and continued each episode to a lower classed working environment. The final working building was a hidden workshop, using kids from the ages of six and above. It also showed the six teenagers returning home to Britain and their changed attitude towards child labour. This also changed my life to a huge extent. I am now a cautious consumer and I research the shop I am considering to buy from.

As a 12-year-old boy I love secondary school but these youngsters don't get this chance, working from a young age for under the minimum wage. I feel they need help and soon. I hope from what you have read in this letter you will see how much people do care about others. I hope you have understood my views fully and seen that I do want to help, along with millions of others, but we can't do that without help. I hope to hear from you soon.

Yours sincerely,
Craig Hendry

# Evan Horowitz

*Japan, Age 12*

### Subject: WORLD HUNGER

Migration is one more reason that thousands of people are going hungry. There are many causes for this migration of people away from their homes or native lands. Some of these reasons are natural like droughts, flooding or erosion of the land, but there are also other reasons why people are forced to move away from home. I mentioned corrupt governments before and this is a big problem. People are running away trying to find safety and trying to keep their families alive. They go to refugee camps where they hope to be protected and given food but this takes them away from their land and so it becomes a cruel cycle of poverty and hunger. In cases where governments are just poor and want to help the people, the best help that developed countries can give is education so that doctors, teachers, farmers can all help to make their communities stable which will then help their country to be safe.

First world countries can help to educate people by providing resources for developing better crops through better uses of agricultural training, improved technology and greater use of land. If the developed countries invest in training then people will be able to maintain themselves and they won't have to rely on help from other countries. There is a term called "sustainable development" which means that it is better to try to help people by teaching them how to help themselves so that the help will last and be passed on to each other.

World hunger is a global problem that doesn't just affect the people who are starving; it affects everyone because starving people are not happy, productive people and the countries they live in are (or might become) war zones full of dying and rioting people. It is much better to have peaceful countries where people are doing well and can be good trading partners with the rest of the world. And for humanitarian reasons it is better to have healthy populations rather than starving ones.

# Calum Watt
*Scotland, Age 14*

### Subject: CLIMATE CHANGE

With everything that's happening around the world it's hard to feel truly safe, especially regarding the important matter of global warming. As a teenager I worry what's happening to our beautiful planet, our home. Every day we hear through the media about how our planet is changing beyond recognition. With the rapid rise in greenhouse gases in the atmosphere such as carbon dioxide and methane this causes more of the powerful sunrays that heat our planet to get trapped within the atmosphere, heating the earth more than necessary. This in turn changes global temperature and changes weather and seasons everyone remembers.

Even my own parents and grandparents remember proper seasons. Cold, snowy winters and long, hot summers. However, that's all changed. Winter doesn't vary much from spring and autumn (fall) and summer is far too hot. Weather has now become more of a threat than ever before. The harsh heat of the sun is too much for countries such as Greece, Africa and Australia. Australia in particular has suffered a lot recently. The bushfires caused by the dry conditions are becoming more common and are affecting both the wildlife and people of Australia. So many lives and homes are lost to the fires. It is becoming increasingly difficult for the brave men and women of the emergency services to try and protect everyone.

The earth is a beautiful place but if we keep relying on old methods and believing sceptics who refuse to accept the existence of global warming and climate change through fear of change then our planet and everything that relies on it every plant, every animal, every person is going to suffer. We could save a lot of gas emissions, money and in the end lives by using alternate energy sources such as wind and solar power because unlike oil and coal we'll never run out of wind or sunlight. Even something as simple as getting people to quit smoking reduces emissions, saves money, improves health and reduces the risks of cancer and heart disease.

If people put their differences and selfishness behind them we can work together as the human race and as friends to build a better world, better way of life and a better future for our children. For them to look back and say, "Wow. They did it. They stopped caring about themselves and started caring for each other and their home".

# Linzi McCallum

*Scotland, Age 14*

## Subject: WORLD HUNGER

The reason why I am writing to you is because I have been doing quite a bit of research about world hunger in class, and to be quite honest I didn't realise how bad it is getting all over the globe. I have found out that many children in developing countries have to go and work to earn money for family needs. It is a fact that 73 million working children are less than ten years old and every year around 22,000 children die in work-related accidents. Over a million people die worldwide each year because of hunger and malnutrition; five million of these people are children. And approximately 1.2 billion people unfortunately suffer from hunger.

All of these shocking fact are true and they really got me thinking how most of us take everything for granted without even noticing most of the time in our daily routines, from simple things like opening the fridge and helping ourselves without thinking about others. Food waste is extortionate, especially in the United Kingdom. A shocking 30-40% of all food is never eaten and in the last decade the amount of food people throw out has risen by 15% – overall £20 billion or $38 billion worth of food gets thrown away every year.

Everyone should be equal in the world and it is not fair on them praying every day, even for the littlest drop of food and clean water – we do take that for granted.

So please help on stopping this problem and make the world a happier place. I know you have plenty of matters and issues to deal with every day, but if you do get a minute, then please take this into account. Thank you very much.

# Brona Murphy
*Ireland, Age 14*

**Subject: CHILD LABOUR**

Ramla doesn't go to school. She used to but had to leave to go to work. She is a bonded labourer in a factory making matches. Her family incurred a debt when her sister Rubina got married and the only way they can pay back this debt is if Ramla earns the money. As she is the eldest living at home she had no choice but to be the one to work. In Pakistan children do what their parents tell them. It will take about four years for Ramla to earn the amount of money required to pay off the debt.

Ramla misses school. She was a very good student. She speaks two languages – Urdu, which most Pakistanis speak, and English. She loves reading. Now and again she still reads if she finds a newspaper discarded in the streets, but her long working hours don't give her much time for reading.

Ramla's day starts at 3.30 in the morning. She has a hurried breakfast of chapattis, a kind of flat bread, and cold water from the bucket behind the front door.

Her working day lasts 14 hours without any breaks. Some days she works until 10.00 o'clock at night but she doesn't get any extra money for this.

She has a dream. She is ambitious. She has it in her head to do something big. Her dreams keep her strong. It drives her forward. When she is thirteen, next year, she is going to secondary school on the one day off a week that she gets. An Irish nun from the order of St. Joseph of Cluny runs a secondary school four miles from her village. Ramla doesn't mind that she will have to walk four miles to get there. And when her four years are up at the match factory she will return full-time to school.

# Sayuri Sekimitsu

*Japan, Age 12*

## Subject: WORLD HUNGER

President Obama, you like trail mix, chocolate roasted peanut protein bars, vegetables, and handmade milk chocolates. You dislike salt and vinegar potato chips, soft drinks, and asparagus. My question for you is: do you know how good asparagus is for you? It has no saturated fat or cholesterol. One average sized can of asparagus would feed five starving children. Think about your children, Malia and Natasha, ages eight and ten. One-eighth of children under the age of twelve in America go to bed hungry. Imagine your daughters going to sleep hungry just because you couldn't supply them with food. Half of all child deaths come from hunger. For the price of one missile, a school of children could eat lunch for five years. The United States of America should spend less money on the military and direct its attention to the immediate crisis, world hunger. The White house has three kitchens and when you have any leftover food, you throw it away. In the last decade, the amount of food in the United States that is thrown away has gone up by 15%. In the UK, 30% to 40% of food is not eaten.

World hunger is like a vine creeping up a garden wall. At first, it wasn't a huge dilemma, but now the vine has turned to be a huge vine with thorns, pricking those less fortunate. Every 3.6 seconds, someone dies of hunger, and three billion people live on only two American dollars a day. Half of all children under five years of age in Asia and one-third of all children in Saharan Africa are starving or malnourished, and one in twelve people worldwide are malnourished! In one day, 100 million children die from malnutrition. With the money the military uses in two days, these 100 million can be prevented. An average American family of four wastes 122 pounds each month, including 24 pounds of fresh fruit and vegetables and 22 pounds of milk. That 24 pounds of fresh fruit and vegetables could feed a family of four in Africa for two weeks!

It takes courage to acknowledge the fact that our world is not a fairy tale but a nightmare, full of hungry and poor men, women, and children. Change is possible, but only if each and every one of us works toward it with the same passion. Every one can help end world hunger even if it is to do such a thing as learn vocabulary words.

# Cameron McClung
*United Kingdom, Age 13*

## Subject: CHILD LABOUR

It is morning now and they have force marched me across the savannah for the whole evening in the chilling, bitter cold. These men show no concern towards me; they don't care if I die. I am just an item, not even the animals are as badly mistreated. When I am thirsty they give me no water. When I fall they beat me and spit on me and when I cry they threaten to kill me there and then.

We have arrived at a makeshift camp where I will learn to hunt and to kill. I am a victim of the raging civil war, a child soldier. If I do not hunt I do not eat and if I do not kill I do not live. I don't need to learn the language I only need to learn three simple commands: 'eat ','kill' and 'march'. I am part of the Ethiopian Liberation Army, or the ELA for short.

I have been training for three weeks now, I am now an efficient killing machine, or so I hope anyway because if I'm not they will kill me for sure. I have my own rifle; it was taken from a little boy who looked no older than about seven.

I am beginning to break under the strain of what is now normal life, I cannot cope with it any more, I am starving, beaten regularly, terribly thirsty and I am given the jobs the older men are not stupid enough to risk doing themselves. In the past few months I have witnessed the most horrific battles and massacres of completely innocent human beings whose only crime was to be in the wrong place.

I am writing this from my deathbed, I was so foolish I did not even look at the ground. All of a sudden I was flying through the air; I was so careless I trod straight on top of it, a land mine. My legs are still out there, no one took them, I will never walk again; the mine may as well have taken my life. I do not want to experience the pain of a slow death.

I now believe what my mother once said: "It is a rich man's war but it is the poor whose blood is spilled."

# Ayumi Akiyama
*Japan, Age 13*

**Subject: WORLD HUNGER**

A friend of our family is a Nigerian doctor who works for WHO (World Health Organization). He told us of his experience in Africa. He met a family during his routine visits to homes to see if there are any sick people. He found a mother sick in critical condition, and beside her was her husband's dead body. Our friend said that he didn't know when the father passed away. Around the parents were their children sitting on the ground, bent and craving food from hunger. The children's ribs and shoulders penetrated their skin and their big bulging eyes looked so innocent to him. Our friend said that he could never forget those children's eyes.

Out of 6.7 billion people in our earth, 963 million people are experiencing hunger. As the new president of United States of America, you are the leader of the world. It is your duty to solve the world hunger problem because the cause of world hunger is poverty. Reducing hunger will solve many world problems like the spreading of varieties of diseases.

As the leader of the world you need to accomplish goals for world hunger one step at a time so the number of people who are in poverty will decrease, several world problems will be solved, and there will be less spreading of diseases.

# Christina Higa

*Japan, Age 13*

## Subject: CHILD LABOUR

Each step is painful and my muscles ache every time I move my body. Even now, as I lay here on the bare ground trying to lull myself to sleep, I can feel the excruciating pain from the numerous times the factory boss beat me with a wooden stick. Every day I have to wake up before dawn, starving and weak from the polluted and ill ventilated factory that I spend sixteen hours a day working in. My back is stiff from having to lean over the spinning-machines that are still running as I manage to move my fingers fast enough to repair the broken threads. There have been many incidents of young children whose fingers and hands were cut off by shafts and other dangerous machinery. I am only one in 250 million children from ages as young as five to be exposed to hazardous environments such as my own.

Don't I have a right as a human being? Why am I getting treated this way for a lifestyle I was born into and had no control over? Why can't I sleep at night without having to worry about how I'll feed my sick baby brother the next day? Since thirteen years old, I never got the chance to run freely, laugh with my friends, make mud dolls, and most of all, be a child. It almost seems as if I was born an adult, having to deal with the responsibilities of an adult, live the life of an adult. All I want is to go to school and learn about all the magical places in the world, the pyramids in Egypt and the temples in Japan.

I've heard that to uphold the dignity of man is the duty of the government to achieve. However this will only happen if independence is gained from good education. The solution to this would be ending child labour, as this will enable children like myself to receive proper education.

As I lay here on the bare ground, something inside me tells me that there is someone out there, a great leader who can help us all out. Before I close my eyes to sleep, I put my hands together and pray.

# Kourtney Easterling
*Japan, Age 12*

### Subject: CLIMATE CHANGE

Let's say you live in an average household. You constantly recycle and try to buy local and organic food, but you still leave your lights on during the day and take a nice, long, warm bubble bath after work. Even if you recycle, carpool, and buy local food you still could be harming the world. Many people forget to do the simplest things to stop global warming such as turning off the light when not in the room, or leaving the water running while brushing your teeth. If you are a person that forgets to turn off the lights, or loves long baths, we have a way for you to still get these baths and to not feel bad if you forget and leave a light on. My simple solution is to replace your appliances with energy star appliances, replace your light bulbs with energy efficient ones, and if you really want to make a simple difference instead of buying a regular vehicle purchase a solar car. By doing these things you could save hundreds of dollars on your electric bill and also save hundreds from not having to purchase fuel for your car. In my opinion, if the economy continues to get worse, if people could still have all the things they normally would and save hundreds of dollars at the same time why wouldn't everyone make these simple changes?

If we don't change now it may be too late and global warming could become worse causing animal extinction, higher annual temperatures, melting cold areas, and other things that could drastically lead to other disasters. If we all work together we can save our planet; let's recycle our old ways into new ones, let's reuse our energy by recycling instead of just throwing out, and let's make these changes for a better life in the future.

# Peter Brown
*Northern Ireland, Age 15*

## Subject: CHILD LABOUR

A Swedish philosopher named Jean Jacques Rousseau once said: "Man is born free, yet is everywhere in chains." These words are perfect for describing the situation in many countries across the world. I am speaking of the many cases of child labour in our society today.

Family illiteracy is also a major contributor to child labour. If parents cannot work because they cannot read or write it may once again be up to the children to support the household. If the children do not attend school then they later find themselves in their parents' position.

However, one thing in particular that I find very shocking is the fact that child labour has been going on for years and that even though our society has evolved and become more equal for everyone, it still goes on! Society has gotten past its racial and sectarian issues, but we are still caught up a world of children being forced to work in harsh conditions.

Now, granted, child labour does not really affect America and it is mainly present in the Middle East and parts of Africa, but your fellow Americans should still be concerned. How would they like the thought of their children having to work in harsh conditions before they are of an appropriate age? Are they not troubled by the idea of little children working all day for what they could make in about an hour?

As Dr. Martin Luther King once said, "Freedom is never voluntarily given by the oppressor; it must be demanded by the oppressed". This is an amazing quote, because it inspires me to stand up for what I believe is right and to not just sit back and take whatever is thrown at me in life. However, for those young children over in Kenya or the Middle East, this cannot help. They are stuck in tiny rooms by people who are much stronger than them, and after months and even years of working in those sickening rooms, they have had all confidence driven out of them. This has forced them to believe that all they will ever do is work and forever be in harsh conditions.

# Meg Itoh
*Japan, Age 13*

### Subject: CLIMATE CHANGE

I never really understood the importance of global warming. I mean, our earth was heating up, but what was there to do? Were we supposed to all stop using cars and begin riding the train? Were we supposed to stop using hair sprays which affected the earth? Were we supposed to begin using solar systems instead of electricity? Yes, we were. We actually should've a long time ago.

We will *face a string of terrible catastrophes* unless we act to pre-pare ourselves and deal with the underlying causes of global warming

You yourself quoted: "All across the world, in every kind of environment and region known to man, increasingly dangerous weather patterns and devastating storms are abruptly putting an end to the long-running debate over whether or not climate change is real. Not only is it real, it's here, and its effects are giving rise to a frighteningly new global phenomenon: the man-made natural disaster."

When I forget to do my homework, my grades go down and I need to work twice as hard to achieve better work. How is global warming any different? Though the climate issue is in a bigger scale than homework, WE started this and now WE need to do something about it.

Saving the world sounds more complicated than it is. Who would've expected that unplugging your TV when you're not using it could save energy, not using some hairsprays which include chemicals bad for the earth could save energy, and who would've thought that if every person in this world *tried* to fix what they created? Saving the world isn't complicated. In fact, saving the world is actually easy.

Saying that, there are six billion people in this world, if every person did something to help preserve energy and to lessen the greenhouse effect, think of how much energy could be saved. Think of how much green there could be. Think of how much the earth would be saved.

People may say that we can't. That we've gone too far. That there's nothing we could've done in the first place, that the world doesn't *need* change. I mean, this is how we've been living for the last couple hundred years since giving birth to high technology. We can't change it now.

But this means we're giving up. We're giving up on Mother Earth which has given us life, which has helped us grow, which has helped us live. We can't give up now. We can save the earth.

Yes We Can.

# Amy Quirke

*Ireland, Age 14*

**Subject: CHILD LABOUR**

I have participated in a child labour workshop so I can personally say that I know to an extent what it is to be like to be a child working as a child labourer. I also know that I have not felt the full extent of what child labourers feel every single day of their short-lived lives. Unloved, worthless, scared, hungry, thirsty, low self-esteem. These are just some of the feelings which they have to get through every day of their lives. The poor children suffering from this exploitation get beaten, abused, tortured, not to mind having little means of food and water.

I was absolutely petrified during this workshop as I was not allowed talk, smile not to mind making eye contact with another human being. I felt the consequences when I disobeyed the rules. I had to walk up and down a hall ten times with my head faced towards the floor. This instantaneously put my self-esteem to a rock bottom and it felt like my heart was shattering into tiny fragment pieces.

The sad thing about what I had to do is that the real child labourers have to do things which are beyond thought. Some of them get battered, bruised, tortured, not to mind some of them dying as a result of these fatal beatings.

Are you telling me, President of the United States of America, that you are going to let this occur while you know it is happening? Did you know that if you took the army out of war for just four days of war you would have created 10 billion dollars! Are you telling me that you are unable to put war off for just four days? If you took the army out of war for five days you would have created an extra 250 million dollars.

# Clár Ní Dhornán

*Northern Ireland, Age 13*

## Subject: WORLD HUNGER

I followed your campaign with profound interest, watching as the race got tougher but never for one moment did I doubt you would win the presidency. Your Irish ancestry, with your great-great granddaddy a native of Moneygall, Co Offaly, may have contributed to your popularity among the Irish voters, and your African ancestry may have contributed to your popularity among the African-American voters, but I know it was your charm, charisma, knowledge and sheer determination that helped win the all your votes for presidency. I would like to take this opportunity to congratulate you on winning the presidency and making history by becoming America's first African American president.

Now that you have settled into the White House I would like to discuss a topic that is very close to my heart and that has been troubling me for along time now. It is happening more and more every day now and I am afraid it might come to Ireland now.

I am a regular tourist to America and over the years I have noticed things that were very disturbing to me. In 2006 I visited LA in particular; I walked the streets of Hollywood and was taken by a family friend to see the mansions belonging to the big stars. This was an awesome day but then we went a few miles downtown and I could not believe my eyes, as the shops ceased daily trading, people in shabby clothes started to gather, some even wheeling their simple belongings in a shopping trolley. Cardboard boxes were laid down in the doorways. The people started to go through rubbish bins and when I asked why I was told they were looking for food to eat. Someone started a fire in a barrel, apparently this was for heat. As people gathered around I could see young and old alike all trying to survive, but a complete contrast to what was available to the people who were privileged to live a few miles up the road.

The first visit to America that I remember was in 2000 when I visited friends in Dallas, Texas, I was five-years-old and I have visited regularly every other year since. But even there things have changed. On my visit last year when I was in downtown Dallas I saw people lying in the streets at night. This was something I had never seen in Dallas before, LA yes, a few years previous, but not Dallas. How can this be?

All these events got me to think about other people and how they survive in various countries. Where I come from in Co. Tyrone, no one sleeps on the streets as there is access to hostels for the homeless or emergency accommodation and no one goes hungry. But I am told we live in a deprived area. Although I am from a single parent family, and to some we may be poor as we have no television because we cannot afford the TV licence, however our basic needs are met in that we have food, a roof over our heads and I have access to an education and my mothers' unconditional love.

So I guess I'm lucky even though I fall into a group of 4.7 billion people who live in low and middle-low incomes, a majority of which suffer from hunger and poverty-related problems.

# Ailish McAteer

*Northern Ireland, Age 15*

## Subject: CHILD LABOUR

My name is Ailish McAteer and writing to you is a privilege and an honour and is making my hands shake at the thought that you actually might read this.

I have never been more in awe of anyone in my life as I was of you as I watched you inspire, encourage, support and reassure millions and millions of people in your history-making presidential campaign. I watched closely with my eager and interested friends as we experienced the ups, downs, highs, lows, twists, and turns of that world-changing election.

In my short fifteen years I have never witnessed such powerful and transforming speeches, I've never seen a man so sure and determined yet not over-confident and complacent, and I have never seen someone strive under so much pressure fuelled solely by a genuine desire to change the world.

Although there is a rare and wonderful aura of hope and optimism surrounding you, your position up on that high pedestal comes with just as many responsibilities as it does accolades. As I am sure you know, there are three major problems facing the world today that need tackling more than anything else. Those three challenges are the current financial crisis, climate change and poverty in the third world. That last one is very broad and unfortunately there are many problems within the label the "Third World", problems that are the consequences of persistent poverty.

The most heart-breaking problem within the third world is child labour. For me the mere thought of children as young as five working twelve hours a day for virtually no money is almost too much to bear.

But I feel if the use of child labour by some big businesses was well publicised then the public would very likely be put off purchasing their goods in that particular store. If a bill was passed stating that all companies that use sweatshops have to state this on the front of every shop the companies will be less inclined to use this inhumane method of mass-production as it would be harming their business to do so.

So President Obama, I know I have given you a lot to think about. Of course I realise that the major problems with child labour in sweatshops within the third world countries are more than just a few suggestions on paper, but I sincerely hope that I have brought to your attention the severity of this issue and the possibilities we have for solving it. This is much needed change and when put into the hands of a capable leader it is "Change We Can Believe In".

# Pia Sen

*United States, Age 12*

**Subject: CHILD LABOUR**

My name is one forgotten, snuffed out, like the emotions my body used to once contain.

I am amongst the few of the enslaved who can read or write, for it is a very dangerous talent to hold – the master fears knowledge, and all that possess it. He wants us to conform, to become one.

Once the sun has long since set, we are allowed to hobble back to the cramped hen house where all twelve of the enslaved are allowed to rest. Sleep eludes us, our arms, legs and back are too sore to allow sleep to carry us off. As we lie down on the crates that form our makeshift beds, the little ones cry themselves to sleep. As the others toss and turn, they ignore the whimpers and try to pretend that they are not crying too.

My life is empty of joy, the only emotions I know are pain, desolation and hope. I don't know how this feeling managed to reach this plantation, a place that does not deserve such a wonderful thing, but all the same it is still there.

I am still hoping that one day, liberation will come, one day; I may be able to walk down the paved road amongst the lucky ones, with my new friends by my side and ribbons in my hair. And in my dream, I will be carrying my shiny new lunchbox.

# Mieke Guinan
*Ireland, Age 14*

### Subject: CHILD LABOUR

In your inauguration speech you referred to the "God given promise that all are equal, all are free, and all deserve a chance to pursue their full measure of happiness". These children, working for less than minimum wage or no wage at all, are not being treated equally. They are not free, they are stuck doing dangerous labour a child should not be doing. These children certainly do not have a chance to be happy. They are being declined their basic rights and they need your help.

Can you imagine being merely five years of age doing full time work in dangerous and excessive workplaces? These children are being subjected to psychological, verbal, physical and sexual abuse as well as working for far below minimum wage or no wage at all. They cannot save themselves. They cannot live the life a young person in this modern era; unless we, as citizens of the world, help them.

Child labour has serious consequences that stay with the child for the rest of their lives. Young workers not only face dangerous working conditions, they face long-term physical, intellectual and emotional stress. They face an adulthood of unemployment and illiteracy. They do not have the chance to be educated, get a decent career, and make a decent living. Many have not survived the inappropriately tough work: 22,000 young workers have died in work-related accidents. In my opinion, this tragic problem in our society should be dealt with soon. They deserve the chance to be saved from the cruel lives they lead.

As president of America, I sincerely hope you will help these underprivileged children.

You could change the lives of all those who so badly need help.

Save them.

# Andrew Leighton
*Scotland, Age 14*

## Subject: CLIMATE CHANGE

There is absolutely no point whatsoever in building up an amazing economy if we don't have a planet. Costs should not matter. We should not have to think twice about this issue. If anything, saving the planet will be great for the economy as it will create a lot more jobs in many industries. The top 10 in-demand jobs in 2010 did not exist in 2004, so you can imagine the amount of jobs created in doing all the necessary things such as reducing $CO_2$ levels, and fixing damage already done.

As the newly elected President of the United States of America, I'm sure you have a lot of responsibilities and a lot is expected of you. The main thing people are concerned about now is the war in Iraq and when to pull the troops out.

However, when all this is happening, global warming isn't just waiting its turn. Temperatures are rising fast and before you know it will be too late. There is no point fighting a war if there won't be a planet to live on. By all means deal with Iraq. Because that is what the people want at the moment. But when the day comes that the earth does dramatically change, people will blame you for not acting soon enough or for not acting at all.

I know there's a lot of pressure on you but global warming is a big problem.

# Caoilfhionn Cullinane

*Ireland, Age 13*

## Subject: CHILD LABOUR

Legislation exists that exploitation of children is illegal. Although some governments and businesses see child labour as a way to keep their costs and prices low.

The question is always asked, "isn't child labour necessary for poor families to survive?" The answer is, no. Child labour should not exist. Families depending on their children's income should be supported and provision of education for the children should be provided.

When children are no longer available to work, employers have no choice but to employ adults.

Child labour denies the basic rights to education and human development for many of the world's poorest and most vulnerable little children.

# Allyson Crosby
*United States, Age 14*

## Subject: WORLD HUNGER

The fire kept me warm through the night as I slept and dreamed. I dreamed a wonderful dream where I had a place to live and there was food all around and I didn't have to go looking for it every time and get sick. I was walking around the house and my family was there. There was food in the kitchen all over the table and I just stared at it for a little bit.

"Go ahead darling. You can go eat." I heard a man say and it was my dad.

I walked towards the food and I sat down at the table. Just as I was about to pick something up and eat it my dream went away, like it flickered off. I was sad that I woke from my wonderful dream. The fire was out but I was still comfortably warm in my blanket. I got up and the blanket fell off of me and a rush of cold air ran through my whole body. I shivered at the cold morning air and picked the blanket back up and covered myself again. It felt good to at least have some warmth but I wish that someone would just take me in and give me some food.

I sighed and picked up my lighter and walked away from the pile of burnt up wood.

# Mario Guzman

*United States, Age 13*

### Subject: WORLD HUNGER

To make you know what hunger really is you would most likely have to experience starvation. I am not talking about when you are hungry and you have someone in the White House to cook you a nice warm meal. Try living a month with just eating one meal a day, having to walk three hours to get a bucket of water each and every day. It's hard isn't it? Although I myself haven't experienced it when I feel hungry I say I am starving and I realized that that is wrong to say because I am not starving I am just hungry, and there are actual people in this world that are dying from starvation. So imagine yourself really starving, almost dying each day, and not only are you hungry but you are trying to fight of diseases, thinking about HIV/AIDS, if your going to die next or if your going to live another day.

I am just saying it is hard and can be fatal. Hunger can cause malnutrition which causes 3.5 million deaths each and every year. That is about one person every ten seconds. You made many promises to the people of your country. I would like if you made some promises to the whole world to give them hope and life. I am not asking for help, I am asking for you to rescue the people of the world that go though hunger and starvation each day.

# Cyril Abraham
*United States, Age 15*

**Subject: CLIMATE CHANGE**

Many deny global warming, denouncing it as one of science's fallacies. However, many people are unaware of global warming's mask: global dimming. Greenhouse gasses are not released alone; rather they are accompanied by soot, ash and sulfur dioxide. These products combine with clouds in our atmosphere, making clouds more reflective thus reducing the amount of the sun's energy that reaches the earth. Why is this so deadly? The effects of global warming are being masked. Without global dimming we would be experiencing the unparalleled ferocity of global warming right now. However, there are other attributes to global dimming. You may be familiar with the Sahel and the drought that was present there. The culprit is most likely global dimming. Ocean currents were altered, affecting the weather patterns, and hence changing the rainfall patterns of the Sahel. Millions were displaced and 50 million starved to death because this sudden loss of livelihood.

Innovation is the solution. Innovation can save us.

If you will remember the old adage, "Necessity is the mother of invention", we can push forward. So many bright minds are quelled before they take root. So many bright ideas are crushed by circumstances. But as the president of the United States you can change that. I recently read an article about a new technology that is in the prototype stage in Japan. Satellites are sent up to space with solar panels and these solar panels capture the sun's energy. The energy is then converted to microwaves and beamed back to earth and converted to electricity. Though there is a long way to go, I was amazed when I read about this. This serves as an example that our environment is an untapped resource of clean renewable energy, why not tap into it? With proper funding and nourishment and above all the cooperation of the human race, we can undoubtedly do the impossible and conquer this problem

# Jenny Ward
*Scotland, Age 15*

## Subject: CHILD LABOUR

I am not so ignorant to say that work for kids is all bad – jobs in shops and paper rounds for older children teach them responsibilities and they can take pride in a job well done – but child labour is taking a "job well done" too far. Shop jobs are safe, fighting wars is not safe!

*I know* that children are the future, they will grow taking seats in government, teaching others, aiding others. Surely if the older generation allow child labour to continue aren't they mucking up their own futures? I know things are improving but by no means are we there. I realise that nothing is going to happen over night but I believe it is not only Americans that deserve the American Dream of which you are to a certain extent a benefactor. How are children these suppose to grow and expand their minds and potential to finally achieve the long-pined for equivalent of the American Dream?

Even in the time you've taken to read my letter another child could have been taken into war ... You are now considered to be one of the most powerful men in the world – in charge of one of the biggest armies in the world. If you gave the order to stop child soldiers within your armies then I know things would improve, the only thing left to do now is hope that you can do something.

---

# Cathryn Gowen
## *United States, Age 15*

### Subject: CHILD LABOUR

---

The children know they are treated cruelly. The bond masters know how harshly they treat their "employees". Their communities watch in horror, yet remain mute. Countries hear about their pains, yet are still.

What did my brother die for, if not to instruct and inform the world? Shall we ignore his shouts from the grave? We know, yet we do not act. How long will it be before the cries of the voiceless reach you? When will it be time to act? When will you prove that you care about children you've never met?

You may ask, well how? The most simple is rioting and banning. Shout with the voice these children never had. No longer buy carpets made by enslaved children. Make sure the items you're thinking of purchasing aren't imported from slave masters.

Spread the word. Make aware their pain. We are their voice. We are their hope. We are their future. I had the opportunity to attend school for several years. I learned mathematics, to read and write, in English, and my native language. I've been given much, and I want to give back.

# Sophie Airth

*United Kingdom, Age 13*

**Subject: CHILD LABOUR**

Today diary, I'm going to give you a tour of my home.

I will start at the beginning, as it is a very good place to start. Firstly there is the door, the deadly door, when you walk through the deadly door you're trapped. When you come through the door you step into the main corridor, it is cold, dark and there are holes in the ceiling.

On the right there is the breakfast hall where no breakfast is served; in fact very few meals are served at all. On the left there is the machinery room. I call it the "chockie". The machines give off so much dust and gas, you can hardly breathe! I have been sent to the "chockie" to work a few times and it always makes me feel sick and dizzy.

Further along the corridor is the stitching room. For hours and hours I have sat and sewed constantly, my fingers usually get very sweaty and sore and so I make mistakes and mistakes means punishment. To go any further than the stitching would be a big mistake. All slaves are forbidden to go past the stitching room. "Master and 'other' workers only," the sign reads.

There are three rooms upstairs. Two rooms are where we slaves sleep. The two rooms are both dirty, damp and both rooms are over crowded. The third room is a bathroom for the slaves, with only one toilet and bath for 90 slaves – the smell is horrific!

This is the end of the tour of my home.

# Sarah Biggin

*Ireland, Age 15*

### Subject: CHILD LABOUR

... the Convention on the Rights of the Child clearly state that a child has the right to "protection from work that threatens their health, education and development", but as we know this right is being ignored in some developing countries. Children are being involved in dangerous work such as mining, factory work or quarrying. Also children may be stuck selling clothing and accessories on the side of the streets leaving them vulnerable to abduction or abuse.

I myself would like to raise more awareness on this issue and help people to get a better understanding of child labour. I think if people had a better understanding on this issue they could work together to help put a stop to it. In some countries children are working up to 19 hours a day and only earning an extremely small wage. They may only work to gain a small income if the parents are too ill or unable to work.

I think many people could help protect these children if new ways were introduced. We could help set up more schools and places where children could go to be in a safer, friendlier environment instead of having their childhood taken away from them. They would achieve their right to freedom and protection.

# Tadashi Nakata

*Japan, Age 12*

## Subject: CLIMATE CHANGE

Some people think that the issue of global warming is just the opinion of others and it's a coincidence that it's happening right now. There is little doubt however that the planet is warming. Over the last 100 years, the temperature of the earth has risen approximately least one degree celsius. The hottest years ever recorded have been 1997, 1998, 2001, 2002 and 2003. If global warming continues, many forms of life will die out and lowlands will be swamped up by water. Do we really want these things to happen?

Many species of plants and animals will become extinct if the earth keeps warming. Over 40% of all living creatures will die because of floods and droughts. The animals left living will have difficulty existing in this new warmer habitat and will also eventually die out. With not enough meat and vegetables, food prices will skyrocket causing a worldwide crisis.

Natural disasters will kill millions of people and leave even more homeless over the next century. Due to the unusual weather, many plants and crops will be affected which will increase world hunger leaving millions hungry and killing even more people. Eventually, all humans could die out due to starvation and new diseases that would occur because of the strange weather.

# Aoife McCarthy

*Ireland, Age 14*

## Subject: CHILD LABOUR

The world as we know it offers chances to most people. However one exception to this is that of the 216 million children worldwide expected to work up to twenty hours a day for a little over a single US dollar. As President Dwight D. Eisenhower once said: "No easy problems ever come to the president of the United States. If they are easy to solve, somebody else has solved them." Child labour is one of the biggest obstacles facing us in the world today, and you as the President of the USA should be striving to abolish this gruesome method of manufacturing.

You stated in your inauguration speech: "all are equal, all are free and all deserve the chance to pursue their full measure of happiness." Of course they do, but this is a non-existent feature of the world we live in today. For the world to achieve this aim, an end to child labour must be seen. For these are the types of hurdles we face as citizens of the world in 2009.

Today, President Obama, I don't write to you as a human rights campaigner, a politician or a woman. No, I write to you as a human being, a citizen of the earth, pleading for you as a fellow human being with the power to help those who need it most. Children, Mr. President – you are a father yourself and imagine how you would feel if your children were being exploited in such a drastic way.

Please President Obama, help Concern and many similar charities, and join the revolution to make child labourers history.

# Part Two

# SENIOR CATEGORY

## (16–18 years old)

### Extracts from President-elect Barack Obama's Speech to the Governors' Global Climate Summit, November 18, 2008

Few challenges facing America – and the world – are more urgent than combating climate change. The science is beyond dispute and the facts are clear. Sea levels are rising. Coastlines are shrinking. We've seen record drought, spreading famine, and storms that are growing stronger with each passing hurricane season.

... My presidency will mark a new chapter in America's leadership on climate change that will strengthen our security and create millions of new jobs in the process.

... But the truth is, the United States cannot meet this challenge alone. Solving this problem will require all of us working together.

... Now is the time to confront this challenge once and for all. Delay is no longer an option. Denial is no longer an acceptable response. The stakes are too high. The consequences, too serious.

Stopping climate change won't be easy. It won't happen overnight. But I promise you this: When I am President, any governor who's willing to promote clean energy will have a partner in the White House. Any company that's willing to invest in clean energy will have an ally in Washington. And any nation that's willing to join the cause of combating climate change will have an ally in the United States of America.

# FIRST PLACE – SENIOR

## Niamh Burke

*Ireland, Age 17*

**Subject:** CLIMATE CHANGE

Dear President Obama,

I really should have begun this letter with Dear Barack. I feel I can call you by your first name because I have known you quite intimately for so long. I have known you all your life. I was the one who allowed you to draw your first breath. I have been with you every day. On your very first day of school, I was there. I attended your graduation. The day you met your beautiful wife, Michelle, I was by your side. I was there that moment you finally decided to run for President of the United States of America. I was present during your entire campaign. I remember fondly the presidential address you made to the large, eager crowd at Grant Park in Chicago during your campaign. If I had not been there, all of those people would have been denied the privilege of hearing those inspiring words. I carried your words out to your people. On the day of your inauguration, when the American flag was raised I kept it flying. I was with you then, and I am with you now.

You and others, Barack, do not realise how powerful I am and what an ally you have in me. Without me, living things great and small could not survive for even a few minutes. They need me around so they can breathe, and they also need me in order to hear. I am vital to the survival of our planet. Without me there is no planet. When God created me, he created me as one of the most powerful forces on earth.

Throughout the history of the world, millions of people have felt the wrath of my power. The worst tornado in US history began in southeastern Missouri, crossed through southern Illinois, and then turned into south-western Indiana. The death toll stood at 625 and more than 2,000 people sustained injuries. Property damage was assessed at $16.5 million, which would be $1.7 billion in today's dollars. The tornado left a 219 mile track, which is the longest ever recorded. It rated an F5 on the Fujita scale. It is not one of my proudest achievements but one over which I felt I had no control. I so often feel that my existence and the course of my life are in the hands of another, more powerful even than I.

There is so much, however, that I am proud of. The relief I give to those under the relentless scorching sun. The smile I put on the face of a mother checking if her clothes hanging on the washing line are dry and finding that they are. The utter joy in the screeches of a child as she watches her little windmill turn.

In the lives of every person, from those who enjoy the privileges and advantages that money brings to those who are stricken with harsh poverty, I am a helping hand. You probably don't realise how much you depend on me every second of every minute of every day. The fact that every living thing on this planet could not survive without me gives me great pride and I am very grateful that I am able to help people in this way, but unfortunately, I feel I am taken very much for granted. The environment in general is, to put it bluntly, collapsing before our eyes. I stand in the middle feeling absolutely useless. Yet, every part of my being cries out to help.

This letter is a plea for your help. I want you to turn your inspiring speeches into enduring action. I want to help the people of our planet in their endeavour to combat climate change. I have the potential to really make a difference. I just need someone, someone like you, to help me realise my dream, because frankly, I can't do it on my own.

I have carried words from your mouth that spoke of change. You are right; change is what we need. It is what we need if we are ever going to help our planet, which, at the moment, is in a state of peril. The polar ice caps are melting at a startling rate. To survive, polar bears must hunt on sea ice and since these sheets of ice are getting thinner everyday, it is becoming more and more difficult for them to find food to eat. These magnificent animals are endangered and will soon be extinct if nothing is done to help them. Glaciers are retreating faster than ever before. Sea levels worldwide are undoubtedly rising because of all this new melt water. Planet earth is disintegrating before us. Human beings can be held responsible for this disintegration. Scientists are certain that human activities, such as driving oil-guzzling Land Cruisers and taking three foreign holidays a year, are changing the composition of the earth's atmosphere. I agree with their theory. You would not believe the amount of disgusting gunk that passes through me everyday. It is a horrible sensation to always feel dirty. I am tired of it. We need a new plan.

The type of energy I could produce is a clean renewable form of energy. It is described as a clean form of energy because of its minimal environmental impact compared to fossil fuels. To help me, you need to insist that the use of wind power is established in places far and wide. Wind turbines need to be manufactured and then set up in areas everywhere. The price of producing utility-scale wind power have fallen by 90 per cent in the last 20 years, and according to General Electric, global prices range between 3.5 and 4 cents per kilowatt hour, making wind competitive with coal, oil, nuclear and gas energy. In some parts of the world, my potential power has already been recognised and I have been put to good use in these areas. I am very grateful for this. However, for me to be most effective, my harnessed powers should be present everywhere that energy is currently being used. It is a very feasible idea that the entire planet could be using energy produced by wind power in the next couple of years. This is what I want, and what our planet needs.

I am offering my help. Please, Barack, help me to help our planet. If you decide to help me, and if this change happens, I will no longer have so much unwanted gunk passing through me every day. When people draw a breath from me, it will be clean and will do them no harm. Nature as a whole will be much healthier and more fruitful. This dream, if realised, could potentially prolong the lives of many seriously endangered animals. It would save everyone money in the long run; countries would no longer have to buy oil or coal. It would definitely create a cleaner, less polluted environment for every living thing on planet earth, and it could help to avoid our planet's ultimate downfall. You and I, Barack, together we can.

Yours sincerely,

The Air

# SECOND PLACE – SENIOR

# Cliona Campbell
*Ireland, Age 18*

**Subject:** CHILD LABOUR

Dear President Obama,

I wish to wholeheartedly congratulate you on your recent appointment as President of the United States. It was undoubtedly a monumental day not only for Americans, but for the entire world. I am confident that you will fulfil your new role as president with the utmost integrity and that you will bring great changes towards improving our currently tumultuous economic climate. However, while media interest appears to be solely focused on our present financial concerns, there is an equally pressing issue that has been going unnoticed.

Sadly, I am sure you are all too aware of the injustices in this world which have been left ignored due to widespread ignorance and greed. One of the greatest inequalities facing us today is the horrifying practice of child labour. As a father yourself, I am sure you too are incensed at the thought of selfish individuals profiting from the exploitation of children. I would like to introduce to you a young woman who knows the horrors of child labour all too well. Her name is Anila.

Anila's fingers work deftly as she sets each glistening piece of glass into the ornate necklace. She is systematic in her work, with the effortless skill of a long established worker. Indeed, she has spent much of her young life confined within the four cement walls of a Gujarati workshop. She is ideal for her occupation – not because of top notch credentials or an impressive degree. No. It is because of her small nimble fingers. Fingers that can manipulate the intricate clasps and gems. Fingers of a child.

The fluorescent bulbs overhead only exacerbate the sweltering heat of the workshop. The children sit crammed along a bench, crouched over their work like old men. Yet their round faces and large brown eyes suggest otherwise. Often they nod off during their shifts, weary from the never ending early mornings and late nights. Western children are woken by alarm clocks and kisses. These children are jarred awake by the sharp slap of their *malik*, or boss. They have all at one stage felt the stinging sharpness of his smacks – if they were late, if they were absent, if they took too long in the bathroom. Anila receives blows around her fat cheeks which rain down on her in punishment for her audacity to ask for permission to go to the bathroom for a second time in her twelve hour shift.

They have heard tales of a place called school. A place where they give you pencils and paper without having to spend a single rupee. A place where they teach you to read the signs on shop windows, the newspapers on the *malik*'s desk, the empty wrappers they must sift through on a daily basis. A place which has gained almost mythical status among the stolen whispers of the workshop. But that hasn't been the life ordained for Anila. Her life is destined to be a constant cycle of endless brutalisation, work and hardship. But she stays, because she knows as a *dalit* she is beyond human remorse. She is below humanity.

Of course, *dalit* is the polite term – the politically correct phrase of those who are trying to be kind. The children have all heard the bad word and it seems to pervade every aspect of their lives – they are untouchables. When they are near those of a higher caste they must avert their gazes and walk carefully so as to not allow their shadows to fall upon others – such an act would be defiling. This is why Anila doesn't dream of anything higher. To attempt to rise above her rank would be insolence of the highest degree. She whittles away her childhood, cutting gems and fashioning clasps for women she will never meet; women in the west who have been blessed by their birthright.

Anila is only too aware of her motivation to complete each gruelling day. If she didn't have an incentive to spur her onwards, she isn't sure if she could withstand the deep slices from her knife, the fragments of glass that imbed themselves into her small hands, the machines that cause vicious blisters to erupt on her fingers.

She does it for all those sepia-tinted bottles with the letters she doesn't understand. She has never learnt to read. Or count. All she knows is that these bottles allow her mother, her *Maata*, whose cuddles and kisses make her feel human again, to rise in the morning and hobble through the narrow lanes of their bustees, where the corrugated roofs gleam in the morning sun and babies wail on the red earth with mothers who can't feed them and fathers who are dying from silicosis in the local mine. For her *Maata*'s little bottles she, Anila, must endure an exhaustive twelve hour shift to receive a daily wage of 50 rupees. That's $1.25 – seven times lower than the hourly rate of an average American on the minimum wage.

Of course, Anila's employment is technically illegal, but this is a concept that doesn't enter the minds of those seeking the largest workforce, the largest output and the largest profit. Sometimes the child workers catch a glimpse of men in suits with big black briefcases approaching the workshop, but they are swiftly ushered into the bathroom. The stinking filth of the toilets is enough to make them retch, but often they must stay there for hours as the *malik* is quizzed and the men with the sharp slaps take up position around their work, fumbling comically with the little jewels in their large clumsy fingers. Oftentimes, as Anila cuts the gems of the necklaces she can see many Anilas gazing back at her in the glittering jewel. All of them have the same weary expression. The expression of a little girl, whose childhood has been sucked from her, only an empty shell left in her place.

She has heard snippets about a man in the west with big hopes and ideas through the *malik's* cracking radio. A man who promises to change the world. A man who says he can. Yet it all seems so far removed from her life in Gujarat. She wouldn't dare raise her hopes in thinking he might whisk her away from the harsh daily toil that is her life. Oftentimes, as she gazes along the glimmering corrugated roofs of her slum, she wonders if life could have been different if she had been born in the west. Would she be the recipient of the elegant drop earrings, the glitzy bangles, the tear drop necklace? Yet, as her mother's wheezing fills the shack, she knows it can never be. Because she was made in India.

Sadly, Anila's story isn't unique. Officially, India has 12.6 million child workers – the world's highest number – but activists say the actual figure is at least five times greater. Many of those employed are as young as five years old. While a host of international treaties and domestic laws ban child labour, the Indian authorities rarely enforce them and because America, like many other developed countries, increasingly import their goods, it too is complicit in the brutal system which exploits these innocent children.

Every year, two million dollars worth of child labour-produced jewellery is imported into the United States from India. President Obama, child labour isn't a cause, it's a crisis, and the crisis isn't looming, it's already arrived. I am aware that the eradication of child labour will be no easy feat, but if I didn't believe like you in "Yes we can" I wouldn't be writing this very letter to you today. Despite her hardships, Anila never stops dreaming. When asked what she hopes for, she smiles weakly. "I hope that in my next life," she says softly, "I'll be reborn as an American."

Yours sincerely,

Cliona Campbell

# THIRD PLACE – SENIOR

## Soracha O'Rourke
*Ireland, Age 16*

**Subject:** CLIMATE CHANGE

Dear President Obama,

It has been a year of dreams for you so far. Your face flickers on every cable channel, graced the front pages of millions of newspapers, plastered on to billboards and buses. Your name has been mumbled from everybody's lips, echoed through microphones, aired over radio. Children could identify you in a picture, like a hero or a legend comparable to Mr. Santa Clause himself. Don't worry, you don't intimidate me. I am not worried by your accelerated rise to fame, your presence does not threaten me nor budge me an inch from my comfort zone. I rest assured in my self confidence that I will always be more powerful, more imposing, more well known than you. I have touched more people's lives, shaken hands with every member of the globe who I manage to meet with every single day, of every lunar cycle of every year.

Unlike commuters to work, who sit idly and impatiently in traffic jams, tapping their fingers on the dashboard, honking their horns and swearing under their breath, the corners of my thin black lips curl into a smile each morning at rush hour. My eyelids close in ecstasy as I inhale my favourite perfumes of nitrogen oxides, sulphur oxide not to mention the carbon, a bouquet of my favourite scents. But it is the little extras that are my luxurious treats, the dark puffs from the poorly maintained engines. The lead that is spit from those grey dusty exhausts is the cherry on my cake.

I am the black dancing vapour that circles the long factory chutes. That hovers over bonfires, twirls around chimneys, pirouettes along the fireplace. The coal is my mother; the turf is my father; peat and oil my sisters. We are connected, we are one and they fill me the fuel that I need. I am eternally grateful to my family, without them I am nothing. The crackling of the fire is the tune that I spin to, that releases me with my friends the fumes that I told you about earlier. As I float purposely higher in the clear unending sky I mingle with my comrades as we laugh and giggle at the fun we will have later. So much can be done from here, it's hard to choose, I want to do it all.

I am the one who now sprinkles the soot, the fine icing that I've made, my own little garnish over the delicate trees, their precious green leaves, however will their stomata work when they are clogged, oh it's such a pity. I am the rugged winds that carry the dirt particles, my precious diamonds, the assortment of whirling hazy gases, the boas of smoke from their commercialised points of origins, across vast oceans, over pointed mountain peeks to foreign lands, sometimes Asia, Africa, China, India, Thailand – these are only some of my favourites.

I am a baker, mixing my ingredients with some water, kneading a soft fluffy cloud of acid ready to fall as precipitation. I am amused by the way the toxic substance burns the roots of the people's plants, crops and fruitage, leaches their once rich brown soil, and wipes out their produce that they base their lives around. I smirk at the dirty children in torn rags that drink the water that I have infected, the twist of their features at its foul tasting flavour, the churning in their stomachs, the scald in their winding intestines, the diarrhoea that's brewing. I laugh at the men who attempt to put food on their tables, who stand in the baking sun whipping them all through the day, knee deep in water, net at the ready. My homemade liquor has transformed crystal clear lakes where fish used to frolic into green, murky pools with a Clingfilm covering of algae. All in a day's work.

I am in charge of the Earth's central heating; it is I who turns up the dial, angles the sunbeams through those gaps in the ozone layer until I can smell the waft of the burning earth, witness evaporating streams, rivers and creeks, see flames devouring crops. Oops, I must have forgotten to rewire the sprinkler system. It tickles me pink to watch them begging for water, dry mouths, dehydrated to insanity. Many can't last a few days in my moistureless sauna, and those that do wish that they couldn't, would rather be buried. I am pleasured when those families go to bed hungry, their stomachs in knots, quivering in pain, and can't sleep with the ravenousness. The screams of the orchestra of babies is my compilation of Mozart's most fabulous creations. They are my favourite to watch, so tiny and little and miniature, just like the size of the pits that they eventually end up in.

When I'm feeling a bit giddy, and want to fool around, I break up this pattern of droughts. I paint the skies a thunderous, foreboding shade of ebony, illuminated by electric jolts of blue and yellow neon flashes, accompanied by a symphony of growls and rumbles. I call together the shoals of overcast and grant the prayers of the people, I give them rain. I spit heavily at them, sensations like bullets against skin, indenting the baron earth, stripping apart whatever sparse vegetation is left.

Pitiful dribbles called streams fill, river banks swell and burst until powerful flood waters terrorise the war stricken, poverty-filled, and developing nations. Homes, barns and shacks are dragged away; livestock engulfed in the merciless tides; children ripped from their shrieking mothers arms, separated, alone. Trenches that hold sewerage invade streets, rush under doors, lap and splodge at their ankles and feet. "Water, water everywhere but not a drop to drink", unless you would like some typhus or cholera with your order. And then the veil of cover rolls back and the sun reclaims the position of power once more.

When I'm bored I blow at their over-cultivated soil, peeling away the luscious green, grass cover and unprotected topsoil. I gesture my long pointy finger at the earth's dessert in an inviting motion and stare at the approaching sands, encouraging them to spread slowly outwards, swallowing valuable farmland, grazing areas and fertile food producing fields. The Sahel region in Africa is my prised masterpiece thus far. I delight in watching the thick, robust cattle and sheep wander in confusion searching for their appetising meals. Watching their plump, firm muscular builds diminish to sagging flesh and bone, mirroring the frames of their shepherds and farmers gives me an indescribable tingle in my midsection, until they become nothing but ant food, worm feed, vultures plucking whatever meat can be salvaged from their carcasses.

The same is true for the natives. I love to watch them shrink in size, their hope, their spirit. They have no dreams, no unique unusual goals or aspirations. No future plans; they won't be lawyers, or chefs or teachers. They just ponder the probability of feeding their families the next day. Toddlers' matchstick legs buckle with rickets, so unnaturally shaped, just look at their laughable bow legs. I run my hands along their chests, counting their visible ribs with my fingertips, it feels glorious. Their bloated tummies, a sign of worms and malnourishment, ridicule their shape even more; I shake my head at their lack of proportion. Their jagged, sharp shoulders protrude their tanned, mud-caked skin creating open wounds encrusted with puss, infected green substances oozing and bubbling, complete with a reeking stench of an odour.

Their round skulls sit securely on their pole like bodies, the lollipop effect. I bet if I flick their heads they'll bobble back and over. I stand back and examine my beautiful scene and my magnificent human sculptures. It is all mine, I am accountable, the creator looked upon his art, and it was good.

My actions and efforts have never gone unnoticed; I am mentioned most evenings on the news broadcasted into cosy, warm living rooms, biographies of my legacy printed in countless magazines and papers read by men in sharp business suits drinking strong coffee, and I am even honoured to be the topic for many writing competitions, university debates and literary discussions.

I have many names throughout this vast ever changing world. Scientists have researched me labelling me global warming, students write essays on me entitled climate change, but to those people that know me best, witness my wrath first hand, absorb the shockwaves of my fury, drink the tears of my frustration and bathe in my unstoppable strength, neither of those nicknames are correct. To them I am called the Grim Reaper. There is no escape; I will collect them all.

Care to challenge me, Mr. President?

# SHORTLIST – SENIOR

# Guy King Hall

*Ireland, Age 18*

**Subject: WORLD HUNGER**

Dear President Obama,

I firstly must offer you my congratulations on your outstanding success in the presidential election. The manner in which you presented yourself and your proposals really inspired me and many others. You have earned our trust and we believe you are the man that can change the world.

Mr. President, you do not need me to remind you that the global economic crisis, which presently ravages our financial institutions, is at the forefront of all our minds. However, we are, and have been, for a long time now, in the midst of another crucial problem which affects 923 million people worldwide. This dire problem is world hunger and it is vital that it is addressed sooner rather than later, before it has tragic consequences.

Every 3.6 seconds someone in the world dies of hunger. We must act before this epidemic multiplies. I urge you to be groundbreaking, to be a pioneer to rectify global hunger. This issue deserves space in your agenda every day of the year. You need to tackle global hunger with the same vigour that you have embraced the financial crisis.

Society today faces many problems with the global food crisis. Hunger and malnutrition are direct results of the lack of food. However, Mr. President, there are three important facts that you must also take into account. Firstly, the lack of food also breeds civil unrest. Citizens in poverty stricken countries exert their anger at the powers-that-be in search of a resolution to their problems. Secondly, starvation can also lead to mass migration. Driven by chronic hunger, people move in search of a better life. And finally, the competition for food and water could possibly overtake competition for oil in both severity and significance.

The Indian subcontinent has nearly half the world's hungry people. Africa and the rest of Asia together have approximately 40% with one-third of those in sub-Saharan Africa being malnourished. I am sure that these facts strike a chord with you, Mr President. Your African roots have been well publicised. With family in Kenya, I cannot comprehend how it would not be a primary thought in your head to help the natives who suffer deprivation every day in your grandmother's country. The rise in food prices in developing countries, such as Kenya, will surely spark unrest. A hungry man is an angry man and an angry man can become violent. Despair slipped into anger and violence last year with more than 30 riots around the world due to hunger. In Haiti, 20 people were killed and a prime minister was driven from office.

With $1 trillion being generated to bail out our banks, is the request for $30 million to rescue our hungry not also a necessity? This could cure short-term hunger in tandem with a view to the future with improvements in agriculture production.

Another problem which arises from world hunger is mass migration. As the global recession reaches the underdeveloped countries there will be a chain reaction. With less money available to the governments of the developed world much needed aid to the countries of the developing world will be reduced. Populations of hunger-stricken lands will be forced to flee in search of a better future.

The thought at the centre of the minds of these migrants is their children, the next generation. These children are lost to their homelands. Hunger saps the life out of their chances to fulfil their mental and physical potential in their own countries. These children, if well nourished and well educated, could be the leaders of tomorrow in their politically unstable homelands. However, due to starvation, they are denied the chance to become part of re-building their societies.

The significance of food and water will make its mark politically in the next decade. The struggle for theses two staples of life will eventually overtake competition for oil. This is highlighted in less developed countries where land is devoted to crops for fuel in place of crops for food.

We need to change our focus and assist the malnourished. Expenditure on our militaries could be cut to use the money elsewhere where real battles rage, where a war can be won. For the price of one stealth missile, a school of hungry children could eat lunch every day for five years. Throughout the 1990s 100 million children died from illness and starvation. Our priorities seem to be seriously wrong.

According to the World Health Organisation, one-third of the world is well fed; another third under- fed and the last is starving. Yet the problem of dire poverty is not confined to developing countries. This issue is also closer to your home. In the US, one out of every eight children under twelve goes to bed hungry.

Mr. Obama, you take to the White House with the highest approval rating of any of the last four presidents. According to a *Washington Post* poll, you are almost four times more approved than your predecessor. Much faith has been placed in you. You are the chosen one and many followers of yours worldwide would be in agreement if you were to place world hunger as a top priority. You have been given a unique chance to break the trend of ignorance and to save millions of the world's citizens from death by starvation.

I firmly believe that the war against global hunger can be won and it would be comforting to hear that you believe it too. Let me echo your words on this St Patrick's Day: *'Is feider linn'*. 'Yes we can'.

Yours, in hope,

Guy King-Hall

# SHORTLIST – SENIOR

## Shane Gibbons
*Ireland, Age 17*

### Subject: WORLD HUNGER

Dear President Obama,

Congrats Barack! You made it to the White House. Is it everything you imagined? How's the food? Any leads on Lincoln's treasure?

I'm sure you're exhausted after such a long and brutal campaign. Trekking from North Carolina to Washington State every week must be tiring. You even managed to overcome both Hilary and John in the process. Again my congrats, Barrack. You're some man for one man.

However, it is my duty as denizen of this planet to inform you that the easy part is over. The hard-graft is yet to come. Economic crash, global warming, child labour problems and of course top of the list, food shortages. I don't think you could have picked a worse time to assume office. You still saying, "Yes we can" in the face of such obstacles?

I hope you are, Mr Obama because believe me we need you, more than you'll ever know. The world called for a hero and you answered your blackberry. Now let's hope you don't lose the connection!

I appreciate that your job isn't easy and expectations are huge. I understand that. My aim is simply to ensure that the main problems are not left at the bottom of the pile. My aim is to promote the issue of world hunger at a time when other problems are more prevalent. My aim, Mr Obama, is to convince you to act against this terrible, intangible beast that is starvation. Every day thousands die as a result of this monster. Okay, stocks may fall and temperatures might increase, but can you really put a price on a life? No we can't.

In your inauguration speech you said, "all are equal, all are free and all deserve a chance to pursue their full measure of happiness". Surely that does not only apply only to American citizens? How are the street children in Mogadishu or Calcutta any different to sons and daughters of Ireland or America? They all deserve equality, freedom and the pursuit of happiness. Every year 15 million children die of hunger. That is three times the size of the population of modest Ireland. Imagine the effect it would have in your homeland if Ireland ceased to exist? As a son of Moneygall yourself, I'm sure you would be devastated if such an event were to occur as would the majority of the population in Boston and New York who have Irish relatives.

That is the sad reality for many of America's finest citizens today. There are 35,760 Somalis living in the USA today. According to the Food Security Analysis Unit, 3.25 million of their compatriots need humanitarian assistance. This picture gets even more bleak when you consider that one in six children under the age of five is acutely malnourished. It is impossible to imagine how these American Somalis must feel. They live in relative comfort and security while their friends and family perish at the hands of hunger. This is a shocking situation and it is our duty as people to try to improve it. You are a symbol of hope for millions of African immigrants. You must act.

The world is aware of you profound love for your two angelic daughters, Malia Ann and Natasha. Your ability to balance family life with that of the world's foremost problems is inspiring. I can only imagine the joy you must feel tucking them in at night, praying to God that they will remain comfortable and safe. Now, can you imagine what it must be like for a parent to tuck in their child knowing that they go to bed hungry every night? Wh..t a feeling of hopelessness for the child and shame for the parents. This is the sad reality for one in eight children under the age of twelve in the US. In the greatest country on Earth, we still have children going to bed hungry. But for the grace of God little Sasha could be in that position. So could any of us.

Since December 2007, 3.6 million people have become unemployed. I'm sure a man in your position is aware of this. It is a staggering statistic, which should be resolved as soon as possible. But what is so much more heartbreaking is the fact that 800 million people suffer from hunger and malnutrition, nearly three times the population of America. You are a democrat Mr. President. You got more votes than John McCain, therefore you won. Why are the needs of three million more urgent than those of 800 million?

World hunger is at crisis level. We must act. Cynics will say that people will always be hungry. If you give them bread they will want bagels, a throwback to the words of Marie Antoinette. This is not true. Any one who has seen these problems first hand will disagree. The world's poorest people in wealth are richest in spirit. You give them a loaf of bread, they will never forget your name.

By the end of this decade world hunger can be wiped-out. It is not impossible. With your help we can defeat this beast.

Here are a few practical solutions. Firstly, let us erase national debt. The repayments and corruption from past governments have resulted in a financial squeeze in most African countries. What they receive in aid goes on interest repayments to your Government. Cut the debt and the country will grow. I assure you it will do more for Ethiopia and Somalia than another Live Aid Concert.

Secondly, invest in combating AIDS. Your predecessor, George W. Bush was a pioneer in this field. He promised to ease suffering and delivered. You can continue his good work. If we can expunge this modern plague, we can go a long way to solving world hunger. Much needed food can replace costly medicine. Conversely, it may help ease unemployment in your country. If any doctors find themselves out of work, encourage them to go to India or Africa. I can assure you they would be appreciated.

Before the election, you promised to end the war in Iraq. I salute your intentions and hope you succeed. The war is costly and is draining funds. Why spend money blowing someone up when we can save the money and the lives by helping to end world hunger. For the price of one missile, a school full of children could eat lunch happily each day for a year. What a gift to give a village, the gift of hope.

I am only one voice, Mr. President, but if one voice can change another and that voice can change a room, it can change a city, it can change a nation and that one voice can change the world. You have the world in the palm of your hand. You can make hunger disappear if you truly want to. I know you won't let us down.

Best of luck with everything you do and I really hope you can be the change we all believe in. Tackle the issues of today but don't forget the 800 million people starving every day. We are at a significant junction in the history of mankind. As Shakespeare so eloquently put it:

> *There is a tide in the affairs of men.*
> *Which, taken at the flood, leads on to fortune;*
> *Omitted, all the voyage of their life*
> *Is bound in shallows and in miseries.*
> *On such a full sea are we now afloat,*
> *And we must take the current when it serves,*
> *Or lose our ventures.*

Let us now take this current together.

Thank you.
God bless you.
And God bless the United States of America.

# SHORTLIST – SENIOR

# Ana Flynn
*Ireland, Age 17*

### Subject: CHILD LABOUR

Dear President Obama,

Congratulations on your new post and best wishes for your difficult task ahead, change. My name is Auma, like your sister. I am 14 and live in Kenya. I was taught to read and write by my mother. Two years ago she died from AIDS and since then I must work to support my little brother and sisters. Every morning I wake to prepare a breakfast for my family of scraps from the table of my employers, knowing it is barely enough to keep them going for the rest of the day. Every day I leave our shack in fear that my brother will not be there when I return, that he will be captured by bandits, that my sisters will get injured or ill. Every morning I trek to work on a half empty stomach. Every morning I pass the school yard, overflowing with the happy faces and crisp white shirts of the school children. Every morning those shirts contradict what my mother told me: "you are as good as anyone else".

I work as a serving girl in a rich house. I toil all day in hot kitchens only to serve food that makes my mouth water, to ignorant fat children who pout to get their way. Ungrateful kids who do not appreciate their home, their food, their family, their education, their overall position of good fortune. I am blanked and abused in their house. I bear the brunt of ill tempers and insensitive comments. I am nothing more to them then a shadow that leans against their wall.

After I finish my long shift I walk two miles to collect water to carry home to my siblings. Work ends just in time for me to walk through the parade of children playing in the street and girls my age strutting their new dresses and trying on adulthood. It pains me to see the look in their eye, the look that says they know more than the peasant with the pail on her head. But I know that a new dress does not give you sense. I know that attracting the lustful eyes of a man does not make you grown up. I know that no school book can teach responsibility the way I learnt it. I know that the pain of loosing your mother can send you from 12 to 20 over night. I know that a long day of work for a minute wage, not even enough to feed your family, can knock the dream for new dresses right out of you. I know that having three lost souls completely dependant on you for absolutely every thing can teach you responsibility.

I return home overjoyed to see my brother and sisters, alive and well. Sometimes I bring home an old newspaper from my work or pieces of a newspaper I have found in the street. That's how I know about you and have been following your success. I read these clippings to my siblings and whoever else cares to listen. Your words, like the wind, have even blown as far as our village. Your winds whisper around our campfires. The people talk of our brother in the United States. They talk of his great voice and his mission to change. They say he will not forget his brothers and sisters under the hot sun. The scraps of paper tell me you speak of feeding the hungry bodies and the hungry minds. Well I tell you now my body is as hungry as a wolf and my mind as unnourished as a desert.

I try so hard to teach my siblings what I know but soon I fear my knowledge will not be enough. They have eaten almost every crumb of education I have ever received and they cry out for more. I know that I may only dream of going to school but my strongest wish is to make that dream come true for my brother and sisters, that their childhood will be blessed by an education not burdened by work. Perhaps my brother will be sent to school by an uncle but my sisters stand no chance. "Education should not be wasted on women," my uncle says.

I hope that your winds will blow change to Kenya as well as the USA. I hope that the spirit of a new Kenyatta will once more walk our lands. Once more fighting for a new Kenya, not by killing but by fighting battles of the mind and of society. Bringing changes that will feed our bodies and our minds.

I hope that all in your country will learn to bellow your message of hope and change because you showed that change could come. I hope that some day we might follow in your large foot steps and bring this same message to Kenya, the country of your ancestors, make the winds of change blow up a storm in our nation, like you have done in yours. And when the sand settles we might see; all children with a school to go to, all families with food on their plates, good honest jobs and a lucid, genuine, hard working government to direct us.

Love,
Auma

# SHORTLIST – SENIOR

## Katie St. John
### *Ireland, Age 16*

**Subject: CHILD LABOUR**

Dear President Obama,

When I was born, I was born free and equal into this world. Before I even spoke my first words my future had been written on the streets of opportunity. Why is it, President Obama, that I, like so many more children, was born "more equal" than some?

I woke up this morning, chose which breakfast cereal I wanted from the selection in my kitchen cupboard, chose what shoes to wear and chose whether to go to school by bus or car. What choice did a poor nine year old boy in Sub-Saharan Africa have this morning I wonder? How many varieties of sugar-coated cereals do you think he had in his cupboard? How many pairs of wearable shoes were in his wardrobe? How do you think he made his way to school? Did he go at all? Did he have the choice to go at all?

The world isn't as small as many would think, President Obama (something that's not too hard to believe when you're Irish), so you can probably see how I find it so difficult to comprehend how life here can be so completely different to somewhere like Sub-Saharan Africa. There, some 38% of children between seven and fourteen are engaged in child labour. Every morning 18% of children between these ages wake up, walk past, staring longingly at their peers playing in the schoolyard, and continue on their painful journey along the dirt road to work. Can you imagine being one of these children, President Obama? Can you imagine hearing the door of a dismal, dark sweatshop slam shut behind you, knowing you would not see sunlight for the rest of the day? That you would have to engage in tedious, difficult and dangerous work in the dead heat of a cramped room with the smell of chemicals and sweat burning your nostrils. They are the percentage of children who don't get the opportunity to attend school at all. The national statistics will try to hide it, but this is the disturbing reality.

About one-fifth of the world's six billion people live in absolute poverty and some families rely upon child labour in order to improve their chances of attaining basic necessities. For instance, in some desolate, rural areas families can depend solely on one crop for income and nourishment. How are they supposed to survive if their crops fail?

Child labour is work that deprives children of their childhood, their potential and their dignity. It is harmful to physical and mental development. It often involves intolerable abuse, such as slavery, child-trafficking, forced labour or illicit activities. What this definition highlights for me is that these children are being deprived of their right to an education, and this limits, at a very young age, their future opportunities and those of their communities. I was astonished and disgusted to discover, President Obama, that according to the Global Campaign for Education, free, quality education for all children would cost ten billion dollars, which equals the amount of global military spending over four days.

It frustrates me, President Obama, that a young child who should be outside playing with their friends is sent into a dark, dangerous open cast mine oozing with toxic gases to break up rocks and wash, sieve and carry ore. The effects this type of labour can have on a child's health, especially on their lungs, is substantial and horrific. Nine-year-olds work in the dark, cold underground setting explosives and carrying extremely heavy loads that lead to permanent injury. Why has there been no law enforced to eliminate all forms of this torture? Everyone is completely aware and yet we have chosen to turn a blind eye. It is as if we have come to accept this exploitation as the way things are, as if there is nothing we can do to stop it.

Many attempts have been made all around the world to put child labour laws and acts into place, however these are often not enforced or include exemptions that allow child labour to persist in some of the most common and dangerous sectors, such as agriculture and domestic work. Even in countries where strong child labour laws exist, labour departments and inspectors' offices are often under-staffed and under-funded and so courts may fail to enforce the laws. As well as this, many governments allocate few resources to enforcing child labour laws.

President Obama, you have the power and the responsibility in both your role as an inspirational figure to the people of all nations and in your capacity as the leader of the free world to mould a bright and promising future for the children of the world. The children of regions like Sub-Saharan Africa need your help and they need hope in what are now dark times.

The issue of child labour desperately needs to be addressed and solutions reached. A global, all inclusive law must be introduced so that this exploitation can finally come to an end, and so that the money sharks that have treated these children inhumanely in the past will be brought to justice. Equal and quality education for all needs to be provided to regions like Sub-Saharan Africa as I truly believe that with education will come the end of poverty. It is education that will provide our generation with the tools to conquer disease, such as HIV and Aids and to slow the effects of global warming. These children are put to work in ways that drain childhood of its joy and crushes their right to happiness and hope, and it must stop.

President Obama, I realise that my expectations of you are great, and that I am not the first to write to you with hopes, views and concerns for the world of which we are stewards, but these expectations, these aims, are realistic and achievable over time. I realise that the world is not quite as easily changed as I wish, but I write to you with hope, with hope for a brighter future for us all.

Thank you very much, President Obama, for taking the time to read my letter.

# SHORTLIST – SENIOR

## Ina Ruckstuhl

*Ireland, Age 16*

### Subject: CHILD LABOUR

Dear President Obama,

Stinging watery eyes, fourteen hours since they last rested. They had seen the splendid Kenyan sunrise, then made their way through unbearable dusty hours, and now as the sun was once again saying its farewell to Nyanza Province all they had left were tears. He failed in his efforts to avoid a tear from staining the expensive leather, and dared not look in the direction of his master's glare. The frightful routine of flogging now surely awaited. The polished shoe now possessed an immaculate shine, and his pitiful reflection stared back at him. Eyes of uncertainty. Eyes of despair. The eyes of the eight year old Amali, whose beautiful name so ironically means "hard worker".

President Obama, Amali toils as a domestic servant in your ancestors' native Kenya, in hazardous conditions, hidden from public view behind the façade of a well to do estate. He is only one of the estimated 158 million child labourers around the world. That is one in six children. I am certain that you are aware of these children who are not free to be children, Mr Obama. Children who slave on coffee plantations, labour in sweatshops, are vulnerable to exploitation and suffer abuse at the hands of treacherous "masters". Child labour is the main factor which prevents children from attending school, wasting great human talent and potential.

Five days a week I spend the afternoon sitting over my study, and six hours later on the opposite side of our planet your Malia Ann and Sasha are engrossed in their homework. At these times we fail to appreciate what is for us entirely normal – education. Our whole life is modelled by and stems from our schooling. Why deny a child the life-changing gift of knowledge, simply because they live in the southern hemisphere, are born during a war they did not cause, or are ruled by a corrupt government they did not elect? School must surely be the best place to work.

The whirlwind that is currently racing through western stock markets also dwells within Amali's master. Any minor miscalculation, error or inaccuracy could cause it to boil over. As our unemployment figures increase, so do their working hours. A fraction of your recent $780 billion economic stimulus package could guarantee education for all by the year 2015 ($4.7 billion per year), and in turn greatly reduce numbers affected by child labour. Perhaps Tim Geithner, your Secretary of the Treasury, will disagree with this investment, but we have given you, Mr Obama, the power to step in and ensure change that we cannot only believe in but that can also be felt by the most vulnerable, something the majority, including me, would be willing to contribute to. As Walt Disney reminds us, "Our greatest natural resource is the minds of our children." Mr Obama, can you be their Martin Luther King and end their struggle against slavery?

P.S. Amali's may be a fictional story, however it is an accurate depiction of child labour in today's world.

# SHORTLIST – SENIOR

# Maggie Nic Aonghusa
*Ireland, Age 16*

## Subject: CLIMATE CHANGE

Dear President Obama,

There are many things I feel I should write to you about. There are so many things that need to be fixed or at least changed in some way in this world. America, as the self-proclaimed Leader of the Free World, must lead us to a better future. You have promised so much, now it's time to act. I may only have this opportunity to write to you so I feel the most reasonable topic for me to discuss is the most significant problem facing the human race today: climate change. It affects us all but the most devastating effects are in the developing world. The continent of Africa, which has contributed least to the world's predicament, is suffering the worst consequences.

I spent nine months in The Gambia, West Africa and I saw clearly that if we all had as few carbon emissions we would still have a healthy planet. The majority of families don't have electricity at all, hardly anyone has televisions or fridges or computers or electric cookers. Most people wouldn't dream of owning a car. I'm not suggesting we try to take away these "essentials" from consumer crazy Europe or America, I'm just emphasising that Africans didn't cause the damage. Nonetheless, when I was there I saw the beginning of the terrible results. The people there worry as the rainy season they rely on gets shorter every year. The dry season is getting hotter. The lakes and rivers are shrinking. The land is being desertified. On average across the continent temperatures are expected to rise by up to 2 degrees by 2050. That, combined with an unknown decrease in precipitation, could destroy all Africa's chances. There are no big businesses or factories in The Gambia, the people depend on agriculture and market gardening as a source of income or merely to feed their families. Needless to say, without fertile land and fresh water they have nothing. Gambians are lucky; the River Gambia runs through the country but even this lifeline is diminishing.

Is it not clear enough yet that we must act? We should have listened to all the scientists who warned us of these possibly dramatic temperature increases, the melting of the polar ice caps and the potential natural disasters long ago. Your would-be predecessor, Vice President Al Gore, made a whole film about these consequences in 2006 but what has America done about it? You, as the Leader of the Free World, should be the one to make the first major move. Your policy as regards climate change should be altered completely. We need to stop climate change in its tracks for the sake of the entire planet. Most climate scientists agree that a reduction of 60% of greenhouse gas emissions is needed to stop global warming, but your country won't even accept the 5% cut required by Kyoto. The future health of the planet is most certainly more important than your economy.

I can see several simple actions that could be taken in your country and set an example to the rest of the world. You could ban ordinary, incandescent light bulbs so people would have no choice but to use CFL bulbs. If you're too chicken to try that well you have the hope of the earth behind you so courage should be your priority, but you could just put a levy on ordinary light bulbs and let people make the right choice themselves. In a similar fashion you could raise taxes on those massive, fossil fuel guzzling SUVs. Raise taxes on internal flights as well to discourage plane journeys when Eisenhower's interstates are much kinder to the environment. There are other obvious actions that I believe should be taken, like having fuel quotas in your gigantic factories to stop them single-handedly killing our planet.

These measures are only the beginning but they still won't make you popular – nobody likes higher taxes even when they are needed. To make them seem more attractive show that you will use the proceeds to help rather than hinder your economy and get out of this recession. Do you want to be known as the President who acted or the President who promised a whole lot and then got too scared of losing office to do anything?

The nations of the developing world need assistance from abroad to get through the catastrophe that is climate change. I believe the first action that must be taken is the wiping of all debt. Africa owes over $200 billion in debt. How can they fight the negative effects of global warming and pay that off at the same time? These people would also benefit greatly from being taught proper water storage and irrigation techniques. You were able to recover land from the desert in California; what's stopping you teaching them how to do the same? This could stop desertification and save much needed farming land from the destruction of climate change.

Africa is a continent that has had massive difficulties since Europeans first landed in the fifteenth century. Let our presence finally be a positive one. Let's help these nations through the coming troubles so that they might eventually have equal standing to us in the world arena.

Thank you for taking the time to read the outlandish opinions of an Irish girl. I feel that global warming is having disastrous effects in the developing world and help must be given. Please be the leader to take the first steps to lower greenhouse gas emissions and help Africa and the rest of the developing world deal with the problems caused by climate change.

Yours sincerely,

Maggie Nic Aonghusa

# SHORTLIST – SENIOR

# Marian Ni Áinle

*Ireland, Age 16*

Subject: WORLD HUNGER

Dear President Obama,

I am writing to you about World Hunger which I believe is the greatest problem in our world and far out shadows the economic difficulties we now face. In your inauguration speech you addressed the Developing World and said: "to the people of poor nations, we pledge to work alongside you to make your farms flourish and let clean waters flow; to nourish starved bodies and feed hungry minds". President Obama, I am asking you to begin to fulfil this pledge.

On the 20th of January you told the people of America and the world that "the time has come to carry forward that precious gift that noble idea, passed on from generation to generation: the God-given promise that all are equal, all are free, and all deserve a chance to pursue their full measure of happiness". It is time to hand this gift to the people of the Developing World. President Obama, bring "change" not only to your homeland of America but to your father's homeland of Africa.

The countries of Africa are struggling daily to cope with terrible situations. The people are dying as a result of starvation and disease. Mothers cradle their thin babies in little huts at night and let out a long mournful cry when their starving babies' hearts slowly stop. These cries travel across the land and become one with the dry breeze; they have become a part of nature and a part of life in these lands.

How can we let this carry on, Mr. Obama, when the children of the First World stuff their mouths with rich cakes and biscuits while their eyes are glued to the latest computer game? The children of the Developed World must be taught about the lives of these starving children who are beaten in class if their stomach rumbles. Our children need to be taught that every year 15 million children die of hunger.

Injustice flourishes in the Third World and the people are held like prisoners inside the cage of poverty and starvation from which they cannot escape. This prison has been built with the bones of their ancestors who were robbed of their freedom, culture and lives when their countries were colonised. These countries are no longer under foreign rule but their people are still shackled to the First World as multinational companies continue to exploit the natives. "Cash crops" are grown by the simple farmers on the best of the land to satisfy the greedy needs of the people of the First World while the farmer's own food is grown on the less fertile land.

We must ask the world: Is it right that the business men and women who are at the head of these giant companies fly first-class around the world without a worry or a thought of the poor farmer who has to watch their own family die of malnutrition and hunger? Is it right, Mr. Obama, that the people of the Developed World down mugs of top quality coffee when the families of the coffee bean farmers do not even have a drop of clean water to drink. No, it is not right, President Obama.

Conditional aid is something that must be stopped without a doubt. I have already mentioned injustice, Mr. Obama, and I have to stress that it is incredibly unjust, unfair and simply selfish that when the Developed World sends aid to the Developing World we demand food for a lower price! How can the Third World get back on its feet and support itself when every time we send aid for them to take one step forward they end up taking two steps back?! No wonder no improvement has come to World Hunger.

President Obama, as you well know, a large percentage of aid which is handed into the greasy hands of ruling governments in African countries is used to furnish fine palaces and arm young boys as young as twelve years old to fight in the army while their families are dying from hunger. President Obama, close your eyes for a moment and imagine seeing thousands of emaciated people dying before your eyes as their government dines and wines on the finest foods in the most glorious of palaces.

Would you think it right if the state of Ohio or Washington DC were starving and crying for help while you lounged in the Oval Office sipping champagne bought with money sent to help your people? This cannot continue in the Third World and therefore I am pleading with you to implement tougher rules and regulations on Third World governments and how they use aid money.

The Developing World has been exploited, ripped and torn apart for the past two centuries and it CANNOT continue. You are the new voice that the world turns to and you can lead us in the challenge to end World Hunger. Fair Trade and other such brands which guarantee a fair deal for the simple farmers working tirelessly to support and feed their families is a project we must support and develop.

The Developed World needs to be educated about the lives of these farmers struggling in the stifling climates of Africa, South America and Asia. Together, our world, Barack Obama, the world of you and me, needs to begin asking the important questions about our teas and coffees: "Was a woman slashed and beaten while picking these coffee beans?" "Was a child denied an education to pick the cocoa beans in my hot chocolate?" Every 3.6 seconds someone dies from hunger. Did you know that, President Obama? It is time that every single child in the First World learns that figure in school. It is time, President Barack Obama, and you are the man to speak and act first.

As an Irish citizen I am very proud of what my country has done to help the Developing World and I admire the tireless effort of charities such as Concern, Gorta, Goal, Bóthar and Trócaire, as well as celebrities like Bono and Sir Bob Geldof. In order to end the greatest problem our world has ever faced we must unite together and end it together united in a good cause.

The United Nations continues to work hard and UNICEF has many diligent ambassadors and credit and appreciation goes to them on my behalf. You, Mr. Obama, need to refresh the campaign and be the beacon of light leading the Third World through the tunnel of the darkness and despair. Your own beginnings lie in the beautiful country of Kenya. Kenya, Mr. Obama is struggling like many other countries and according to *National Geographic* half of Kenyans live on the equivalent of less than a dollar a day. Kenya is famous for its exports of tea but despite this "big business" the lives of the people are filled with disease and hunger.

You have the chance to change the story of the starving young girl who cries herself to sleep every night knowing she might never wake up to see the red Kenyan sun. The land of your ancestors is calling for help, President Obama. By setting stronger rules concerning distribution of aid, by donating money to be used on food, water, health and education supplies, by supporting faithful charities and by educating the First World fully, I know you can reply with a definitive answer that will change their lives.

Mr. Obama, non-governmental organisations around the world work 24/7, every day of the year, to try to improve and save the lives of millions and their work is the greatest mankind has ever done. Now they need you to tell the world that "change can come", "yes we can" and we can "begin again". The truth is, President Obama, that anything can happen if we only believe. Nothing is impossible.

Sixty years ago almost every coloured citizen in the United States of America would have thought that a coloured man would become President of the United States of America in this century. I say it again: nothing is impossible. As Dr. Martin Luther King was the voce for African-Americans in their time of need, you can be the voice of starving Africans in their time of need. Dr. Martin Luther King had a dream

Think of your own daughters Sasha and Malia. Do you want them to grow up in a world where the people of the land where their heritage lies are dying from hunger?

It will be a struggle, maybe a war, to end World Hunger but it will be the greatest war any country has ever fought. It will save million instead of killing them and you can be our General. I believe that is a world worth fighting, don't you?

The Declaration of Independence states that every man is born free. No man or woman is born free in the Developing World. They are trapped hunger. Let us set them free. Is that not the greatest act we can ever do?

"Be the change you want to see in the world". President Barack Hussein Obama: be that change.

Yours Sincerely,

Marian Ni Áinle

# Passages, Extracts, Quotes
# – Senior Category

# Aisling Toner
## *United Kingdom, Age 18*

**Subject: Climate Change**

Humanity will be divided as never before by climate change, with the world's poorest countries being the consequent victims. Increased drought, crop failure, disease, extreme weather events and sea level rise are all likely to fall much more heavily on struggling developing populations in Africa, Asia, and South America than on rich industrial societies of Europe, North America and Australia, who have done most to cause global warming through greenhouse gas emissions in the past, and who cannot afford to offset the consequences. Even though it is the powerful, more economically developed countries that produce the most pollution, it is the people in the developing countries that are mostly affected by the outcomes of the changing climate, a highly unjust situation. They have to endure the consequences of our actions. I believe with your help, Mr. Obama, and cooperation between other major industrial nations, the extent of these impacts, especially on developing nations, can be significantly decreased.

# Sierra Weir

*United States, Age 18*

### Subject: WORLD HUNGER

I spent one month in Nicaragua this summer on a service trip with Al-Campo International programs. As naïve as I was, I expected visiting a banana republic much like the places my friends traveled to for vacations. I was devastatingly wrong.

I lived amongst local villagers in their leaky mud huts, eating their meager rice portions three times a day. I even visited an orphanage in a village built on Managua's (the capital) landfill. The children sifted through five metric tons of trash for valuable items to resell to businesses. Nicaragua's citizens are all shorter than me, on account of poor early nutrition. I also was fed white bread with minimal nutritional value and Tang soda. Both are viewed as delicacies and cheap alternative staples of their native diets. I wanted to know how Nicaraguense diets went so far astray from their original meals.

The reason is very clear. Nicaragua is a third world country. The Sandinista Revolution left the government corrupt and dangerous. American co-ops and other developed countries offered aid in the form of donations. Over time, the citizens adjusted to these free handouts instead of going hungry. This was detrimental to their health and economy.

Instead of a handout, people affected by world hunger need a hand-up.

# David O'Sullivan

*Ireland, Age 16*

## Subject: WORLD HUNGER

For a brief moment I want you to put yourself in the situation of a starving African family, and the hardships they have to endure because of hunger.

Tau woke to the piercing screams of his sisters crying. He hadn't slept much the night before on the cold hard surface of the floor. He didn't have the energy to get himself up, so he lay there on the floor trapped under his blanket, listening to the haunting screams in the next room.

Tau had not eaten in two days, and had drank little water in this time, as the trip to the nearest well was a four hour walk, and longer coming back because of the weight of the water they had to carry.

His family's last trip to the well had been three days ago and know the water supplies were running low.

His mother was left on her own to look after four children, because three weeks ago Tau's father died from malaria, because his family didn't have sufficient funding to provide the vaccination needed to cure him because they needed the money to put simple things such as bread on the table.

# Megan Sweeney

*Ireland, Age 16*

### Subject: WORLD HUNGER

Here is what a writer in India had to say about hunger from a personal perspective: "for hunger is a curious thing, at first it is with you all the time, waking and sleeping and in your dreams and your belly cries out insistently, and there is a knowing and a pain so sharp and you must stop it at any cost, and you buy a moment's respite even while you know and fear the sequel. Then the pain is no longer sharp but dull and this too is with you always, so that you think of food many times a day and each time a terrible sickness assails you and because you know this you try to avoid the thought, but you cannot, it is with you. When people in the United States go to the food stores they have a choice of thousands of products including fresh meat, fruits, vegetables, and dairy products as well as countless prepared foods. Few nations in the world have these choices."

The world produces enough food to ensure every person a healthy and productive life. At the same time more than 800 million people suffer from chronic malnutrition, while large numbers of people in parts of the world suffer from overweight and obesity.

# Emma Delaney

*Ireland, Age 16*

## Subject: WORLD HUNGER

It is now Lent in the Church calendar. On Ash Wednesday, some devout Christians spend a day fasting. I could only imagine how hard this would be – a full 24 hours without any food. But for some people, this is something they *have* to do. It has nothing to do with religion; it is not a matter of choice. In the US, 11.7 million children live in households where people have to skip meals or eat less to make ends meet. That means one in ten households in the US is living with hunger or is at risk of hunger.

The fact is that there *is* enough food produced in the world. We have the experience and the technology *right now* to end hunger. The challenge we face is not about the production of food and wealth, but more equitable distribution. It would take a modest effort to end hunger and malnutrition worldwide. Hunger is a *political* condition. And so the key to overcoming hunger is to change *the politics* of hunger.

# Carolina Salinas
*United States, Age 17*

## Subject: CHILD LABOUR

So I urge you sir to bring awareness on this global issue. Because I believe that if the world knows they will fell regret and become activists for the many children around the world who are working whether it be like me or children in other countries working in factories, for merchandise which you probably buy. So please, even though it is too late for me, don't let this atrocity continue any longer. The robbing of childhood is in my eyes a human rights violation. I hope you will make this your utmost priority, for the children are the future of this world and if they are born into these conditions they will feel trapped and unable to pursue their dreams. You never know, one of these kids could be the inventor of something revolutionary or the next influential speaker of the years to come.

So I ask you this and only this: what is it that you are going to do to save the following generations of mankind?

Sincerely,
Lost childhood

# Hannah McDonnell

*Ireland, Age 17*

## Subject: CHILD LABOUR

A great deal of attention has been drawn to the global problem of child labour, but we still look up from our dinner plates to the television and comment on how something should be done and yet continue to eat without a second thought to the subject. Many people, when they think of child labour they think of sweat shops, but that is not the only work that many children are forced to do every day. Other things, such as sexual exploitation, are something we don't like to think about but for many small children it is a living nightmare.

The children are sold by their parents to employers to pay off debts or to get more money for the rest of the family, becoming slaves working tirelessly for the rest of their sort lives, developing health problems as they grow in small cramped places.

No one is taking responsibility for what is happening in the world around us. Just about everyone is guilty of taking part in child labour through the buying and selling of goods made across the world, usually in the poor, underdeveloped nations. This issue has been around for a very long time but people in developed nations such as ourselves in Ireland and yourselves across the sea ignore the reality of the abusive conditions that are still a living nightmare to many across the world. This is my reason for writing to you and wanting a change for the better, for the world in which we all live.

# Sophie Rogers
*United Kingdom, Age 17*

## Subject: CLIMATE CHANGE

An example of how climate change affects developing countries is Africa. The continent as a whole is 0.5 degrees warmer than it was in the 1900s; however the reason for Africa's vulnerability to global warming is its economy. The majority of Africa's economy is based on agriculture, which is rain-fed; therefore as water is already scarce, shortages are even more unwelcome.

By 2032 up to 24 countries in Africa will suffer water scarcity. Climate change leads to two main problems in Africa. Firstly, as rainfall becomes more variable, competition for water increases and arises between countries, especially when Africa's largest rivers, such as the Nile, cross national borders. Another problem is that when scarcity increases, so does the dependence on poor quality sources. Unfortunately, this can lead to water-borne disease such as cholera. This then adds to the pressure being put on health care systems and the government budgets.

As your country is the most powerful in the world you would be able to use your influence to make everybody get involved with reducing carbon dioxide emissions, thus reducing climate change all over the world. A way of reducing the carbon dioxide emissions of American and other main areas in the world, such as Europe and the Far East, would be to promote car share or public service usage; this would then reduce the amount of cars on the roads and therefore reduce engine emissions that are outputted into the environment.

# Oliver Glover

*United Kingdom, Age 17*

## Subject: CLIMATE CHANGE

Other LEDCs such as Bangladesh will face different problems if climate change continues. For example, with 60% of the country lying less than one metre above sea level, and the majority of the country being located on the flood plains of the Brahmaputra, Meghna and Ganges, a rise in sea level and increased rainfall during the monsoon season due to climate change will cause mass destruction. The area along the coast of Bangladesh is home to the poorest and most vulnerable of the population and the world. This means that they are unable to cope with hazards effectively and they do not have the technology or health care to prevent floods and diseases spreading when these hazards occur. This situation can only get worse with weather patterns becoming more extreme and the likelihood of cyclones and prolonged wet seasons will increase.

As the President of the most powerful and influential country in the world, it is your duty to this planet to do all in your power to help save the lives of millions in less economically developed countries by reducing emissions and prevent climate change.

Yours sincerely,

Oliver Glover

# Eoin O'Driscoll

*Ireland, Age 16*

## Subject: WORLD HUNGER

Hunger is also directly linked to civil unrest. Simply put, a hungry man is an angry man. To quote a past governor in your own home state of Illinois, Adlai E. Stevenson, "A hungry man is not a free man". Hungry people are desperate, easily manipulated by extremists, easily riled up in anger. Just hearken back to last year's food riots in Haiti and Cairo! A hungry nation is unstable and perfect breeding grounds for yet another third world dictator who, as well as oppressing yet more of the world's poor, would likely threaten US interests abroad.

Of course, it is not just through spending your nation's money that you can make a difference. Mr President, you are the most powerful, the most influential man alive at the moment.

What change would be more profound than ending world hunger and freeing 923 million people from a life of desperation and malnutrition? How better to fulfill your promises of hope than by helping to end a problem endemnic in our world since the dawn of man?

Whatever you do, Mr President, know that it is in your power to bring about real change. By putting aside a small portion of your Federal Cash Reserve, you could change the lives of untold millions. People starving around the globe, impoverished families struggling to put food on the table, hungry children forgoing education to earn just enough to to survive. Mr President, by utilising your country's economic potential your inspiring message of change could resonate around the world and improve the lives of close to a billion people.

Those efforts, however, would pale in comparision to what you could achieve by leading the free world in a crusade against hunger. By leading the struggle, other nations will follow and hunger can truly be made history.

# Brigid Leahy
## *United States, Age 17*

### SUBJECT: WORLD HUNGER

Dear President Obama,

Every five seconds a child dies from malnutrition. In the time it took you to read that sentence a child has died. While this is a morbid and daunting statistic, the reality is: it does not have to be this way. We must stand together now, as a nation, and fight this global food crisis.

Not long ago, a man by the name of Thomas Awiapo came to my school, Saint Vincent Ferrer, to speak about his experiences. Thomas grew up in Ghana and was orphaned and lost two brothers at a young age because of hunger. He told us that he was only able to attend school because Catholic Relief Services (CRS) came to his village and set up a school where students got a snack and a small lunch each day. Thomas continued to go to school and was educated because the only way for him to get the small snack and small lunch was if he went to the classes. He joked that they tricked him into an education by promising him food to eat, but he also admitted it was the best thing that could have happened to him. Thomas is so grateful to CRS to and all the people that donated money to the project that he travels around the world to tell his story. At schools, when he goes to speak to students they sometimes invite him to eat with them; he is so thankful for the students who share that lunch time with him but is always sad to see how much is thrown away at the end of lunch. There are millions of people who would be so thankful for those scraps in the garbage because they do not get enough to eat on a regular basis. In some parts of the world people eat dirt because it is their only option. Thomas' inspirational story brought the world food crisis close to home. He is proof that hunger does not have to end the millions of lives that it does.

# Nicola Pepper
*Ireland, Age 17*

## SUBJECT: CHILD LABOUR

Dear President Obama,

Firstly I want to extend my sincere congratulations to you on your triumph in winning the election and becoming the new president of the United States of America. I want to express how deeply your inauguration speech touched my heart and the hearts of millions of others. "Today I say to you that the challenges we face are real. They are serious and they are many. They will not be met easily or in a short span of time. But know this, America — they will be met." You particularly transfixed with me with this quote. I thought the way you bravely addressed America, with the harsh reality of the challenges we are yet to face, was outstanding.

This brings me to the reason for my writing to you. I personally have a huge interest in the topic of child labour and I want to know how you plan to rid the world of such cruelty.

In 2000, 246 million child workers aged 5 to 17 were the victims of child labour; 171 million were involved in work that was hazardous to their safety, mental and physical health and moral development; 8.4 million children were forced into child labour, engaged in child trafficking, used in armed conflict and for commercial sexual exploitation. These may just seem like facts and figures, but look beyond the number to every child that it represents. Every child has rights – safety, food, warmth and shelter are all basic needs and rights. But look at children around you; they are not worried about their basic needs, because they have them and more. They lead a normal life, learning, playing and growing, not working, being abused or used.

Children who are forced to work at a young age are more likely to suffer from mental and physical health problems in later life. Is putting a child to work for cheap labour worth sacrificing their whole life? I ask you this question not looking for an answer but a solution to this outrageous situation that is occurring day in and day out.

Kids are crying out to be saved and I believe you're the president that will save them.

I wish you the very best of luck in your presidential duties and I hope you will be more inclined to make this a top priority.

Yours sincerely,
Nicola Pepper

# Jessica Zamora

## *United States, Age 17*

**Subject: CHILD LABOUR**

"Grab that axe!" an old grungy man demanded. Habib swiftly took the steel axe in his sweltering blistered hands and flung it into the air to take the first strike at the brick like wall of dirt only to feel the vibration trickle up his arm and send chills down his spine. The man muttered horrid words to Habib with anger and frustration. Habib, only four years old, cried at the torment he was receiving from the merciless man he called father. Every day was the exact same from sunup to sundown. Habib slept in a rundown little shack with practically no walls and a very moist environment. Not the best kind of environment for a child to have to live in. He is forced to go straight to work by his master with no food to feed his hunger. As he works away, the heat makes his ache stronger and more intense. Going through the same routine every day, Habib is becoming part of the percentage of child workers that die. Habib is a child just as you and I once were. What can you do to save this poor innocent child from being a child labourer?

So much can be done in little time. We just need to imagine a better future for the young children that are working so hard for something they do not even want and it will soon become a reality, a reality to those poor children who have nothing to live for. Well let us make it a reality and not just hopes and dreams. Together we can accomplish anything.

The question that must be answered is, when will it stop? When will these children stop suffering? When is it okay for a child to come outside and play with other children of their age?

The answers lie in your hands. You have taken the responsibility of the US nation and have asked for your fellow citizens' concerns on such matters. Here is mine and I know you, President of the United States, will do what is right. Make the change that you have so much stressed.

Better yet, BE the change!

# Eibhlin Browne
*Ireland, Age 17*

## Subject: CHILD LABOUR

Your election to the presidency has been looked upon as a fresh wave of hope by millions of people throughout the world. All through your career you have been making records and setting standards. You were the first African-American president of the *Harvard Law Review*, and now you are the first African-American president of the United States of America. I ask you now to continue your legacy and be the first president to make a stand against child labour and to do all that is in your power to eradicate it across the world. I am honoured that you have taken the time out of your busy schedule to read this letter and I thank you sincerely for listening to my views.

Yours faithfully,
Eibhlin Browne

# Maura Naughton
*Ireland, Age 16*

**Subject: CHILD LABOUR**

First of all, I would like to say that myself and the whole of Ireland are delighted on hearing the news that you have become the 44th president of America. There has been immense support for you and your party over here throughout the campaign so it is great news to hear the American people have elected you as their president. The little village of Moneygall, Co. Offaly has been buzzing with energy and excitement since discovering your old Irish roots there. On that note, feel free to call over any time, there will always be a warm welcome here for you!

As you have strong family roots in Kenya, Mr. Obama, I decided to highlight the country's child labour situation. In Kenya, most child labourers work in coffee, sugar or rice plantations – 60% of workers in these plantations are children! Between 3 and 3.5 million children are child labourers in Kenya, working at hazardous jobs in dangerous conditions. Nevertheless, many other children work in the informal sector, which cannot be easily monitored and controlled. Therefore, there could be anything up to 4 million children actually working as labourers in Kenya itself! Countries like Kenya in sub-Saharan Africa have the highest amount of child slaves in the world. These countries need the most help to solve the deep problems in their economies and societies.

I do not want this to sound like a lecture sir, but it's time to face the facts of the injustices of our world. It is obvious that every country has its own problems, be it economic, social or natural, but it is extremely important that we tackle child labour before it grows out of control.

Maybe you are aware of the "Stop Child Labour" campaign, which is currently working towards providing this needed education to help stop child labour. I think that their slogan sums up their ambitions perfectly: "school is the best place to work". I hope that you feel as strongly as I do about providing efficient education to the poorer regions of our world, which desperately need it.

Thank you for the time you took to read this letter, Mr. Obama. I hope you agree with my views and try to make some difference in the lives of these neglected child labourers. I wish you every success in your future as American president.

Good luck and best wishes,
From an Irish student

# Daniel Clancy
*Ireland, Age 16*

**Subject: CHILD LABOUR**

It's clear that we need to tackle this global plague. Those in authority need to act to prevent child labour. All around the world, the futures of millions of children are being taken from them. Those that gain from the exploits of these children's rights violations should be punished. Many giant multinational companies freely employ children to pick cocoa beans, stitch branded sportswear and manufacture toys. They are quick to distance themselves from this and are rarely reprimanded. It is mainly us in the developed world that benefit from such crimes and violations. It's time that we take a stand against countries which permit children working at an age when they should be educated and cared for. It's time that we take a stand against countries that tolerate illegal child exploitation, that allow children to be used to solve debts. It's time we see change in that attitudes of backward thinking states. Why should the young and vulnerable be subject to inhuman working conditions, a lack of education and a life-long endurance of hardship and poverty? We need to act, now!

It is at this point that a finger of responsibility points towards you, President Obama. Being one of the most powerful and influential men on this planet, the wand of change is in your hands. You have promised change and hope to the people of America and they have chosen you to lead your great nation. So I now ask of you on behalf of the people of the rest of the world, on behalf of the 218 million child labourers, on behalf of all those who have suffered and perished in greed and cruelty, to deliver change, to deliver hope, to deliver a world with zero tolerance for child labour and rights violations.

The time to act has arrived, President Obama.

# Jennifer Gargano
## *United States, Age 16*

### Subject: CHILD LABOUR

… Growing up in Los Angeles, I certainly have seen no shortage of poverty. And occasionally on some Saturdays I do "my part" and help out with an organisation that makes lunches and delivers them to the poor in Los Angeles. And even my school participates in those canned-food drives and donates money for charities. But even with everything being done by numerous schools, organisations, parishes and volunteer groups, there has been hardly any change in the condition of those who go hungry.

While everyone can hope that a change will occur, unless the country, the continent, the world, acts in solidarity, there can never actually be an end. We focus on the small unimportant things in life and leave the big important things out of our minds. And many people are discouraged when they hear of the exponential number of men, women and children suffering, questioning themselves, "How can I even make a difference?" But these are the attitudes that "feed hunger", a sense of hopelessness which can lead to a lack of action. With all due respect, I believe that world wide poverty is an issue that has been overlooked in the eyes of the United States. Being one of the, if not *the*, wealthiest, strongest and most influential nation, our actions, or really our *inaction*, affects other nations.

We need to step up to the plate and take action, whether it be more aid from organisations like the Peace Corps or monetary donations. It needs to happen. While in the past, aid to poorer nations has sometimes proven to be ineffective, there are some success stories in which countries have significantly reduced poverty, and therefore hunger, and moved from dependence to self-reliance.

Hunger is affecting millions all across America and throughout the entire world. This issue may be one of the greatest challenges of the twenty-first century, but eliminating world hunger truly is a top priority. Please, be the president that steps up and aids humanity, and our beloved country, for the better.

Sincerely,
Jennifer Gargano

# Michael Magee

*Ireland, Age 18*

### Subject: CLIMATE CHANGE

In 2005 Hurricane Katrina, a category five hurricane, hit American soil and claimed the lives of 1,836 people. The storm is estimated to have been responsible for $81.2 billion in damage. Mr. Obama, action needs to be taken to fight climate change so that extreme weather events, such as Hurricane Katrina, do not become a regular occurrence.

The average American generates about 15,000 pounds of carbon dioxide every year from personal transportation, home energy use and from the energy used to produce all of the products and services Americans consume. In order to reduce this staggering statistic there needs to be reform in the American economy.

The solution is to build a clean energy economy. Many governments have shrugged at the idea of a climate change crisis because of the large capital expenditure required to deal with the problem. Governments have viewed it as simply not economically viable. Governments believe that they should allocate their limited resources to more productive areas. I disagree with this view. In this period of economic instability climate change is an opportunity for governments to rebuild their economies. Climate change opens up a new industry for economies around the world, a green industry. This industry will comprise of new innovative companies who will strive to make businesses' production processes more environmentally efficient, provide efficient alternative energy sources, and reduce the carbon footprint of each household.

In order to kickstart the fight against climate change, a few simple policies should be implemented. Mr. Obama, you need to bring in regulation that ensures that contractors are building for energy efficiency. In the United States alone, buildings are responsible for 25-35% of greenhouse gas emissions.

By making simple changes, like using the proper amount of insulation, half of the energy it takes to power buildings can be saved. An effort also needs to be made to cut fuel costs on the road. $CO_2$ emissions from cars and trucks account for about one-third of all energy-related global warming pollution in the United States. Cars bought in the United States last year averaged only 20 miles per gallon, which is less than half the gas mileage available on the most efficient cars today and about the same as a 1908 Model T.

---

# Gerard Mullane

*Ireland, Age 16*

## Subject: CLIMATE CHANGE

---

I am writing to you for a number of reasons. Firstly, I must say congratulations on your inauguration. This is truly history in the making and I am delighted I am alive to witness such a historic event. I am sure your presidency will lead the world into a new era of peace and understanding.

Now I am afraid I must get down to business. The real reason I am writing to you is to talk about a deeply disturbing issue which affects our entire planet. That issue is climate change. It has been staring us in the face for too long and we can no longer sit idly and watch as our planet is destroyed. People talk about how there is nothing we can do to stop this from happening, but these are the words of cowards who hide from the problems they have created.

I feel certain that you, President Obama, will make a stand and force the people of this planet to admit their shortcomings and take positive steps to putting this world back on the right course.

You may think I have written this letter to criticize the human race but this is not true. I have written this letter to warn you of this future scenario. I hope that in your new position of power you will finally open the eyes of the world and take some simple steps to finally change these impending problems. They may seem to be impossible to overcome, but with a few simple steps I'm sure that together, the human race can stop this and build a brighter future.

President Obama, I am sure you realise these very clear and present dangers and it is my deepest wish that our planet can be saved by making a few small changes to our lifestyle. I hope we can come together as a civilisation and stop this change once and for all.

Yours sincerely,
Gerard Mullane

# Jessica Leen
*Ireland, Age 17*

**Subject: CHILD LABOUR**

Dear President Obama,
Most sixteen-year-old girls don't appreciate it when other people read their diaries. I am however in a different state of mind to

those girls at present. I would very much appreciate it if you took time out of your busy schedule to read the following entries. Thank you.

*Susan*

Dear diary – We made it! Another school year behind us at last! Mom's refusing to help me out any further with my frequent fashion bills. I mean I'm only sixteen for crying out loud, what am I supposed to do? I'm hardly capable of establishing some world dominating Business Empire with the fruitless seventy euro and thirty four cent I call my piggy bank. No, I'll just have to settle for something less intricate. And now, to add to my current predicaments, I can here my mother calling in demand of my house cleaning services. Why can't I just be free? No chores, no work, no money problems.

*Lyn-Song*

Dear diary – I couldn't sleep last night. A million and one troubled thoughts circled my mind, each burning with its own distressed fire. What if the factory is shut down? Where will I be left? How will I feed my brothers and sisters? It's not easy to find work like what I have now. Since the age of five I have been casting silk scarves, denied of any alternate life. The childhood I cannot claim is awash with memories of sewing, stitching and heedless weaving. I did not ask for this. I did not ask for each living hour of my existence to come teeming with complications that are not meant for young hearts.

*Susan*

Dear diary – So I found a job. It's nothing amazing, but it certainly feeds my bank account! Ten euro an hour is not too bad, I must say. I mean, it's nothing compared to the handsome fifteen and twenty that my friends are earning, but it'll do. I basically stand by the dressing rooms and criticise customers on their repulsive clothing choice!

### Lyn-Song

Dear diary – I don't know how much more of this I can take. After a sixteen hour day you would think my tired hands and worn eyes have seen enough, but this is certainly never the case. Where did my youth go? Did I ever have one? No, it was taken from me, stolen. And in its place was left a lifetime supply of long days. It's always a long day.

### Susan

Dear diary – I am so ashamed. I am utterly disgusted with myself. How could I have been so selfish? Every day I wake up and I complain. I complain about everything and anything I think is wrong or unfair in my life.

I found a letter today, a diary entry more like, I found it by mistake. A package of those beautiful silken Chinese scarves came in to the shop and it was my job to put them out on display. Whilst unravelling the bewitching cloth of a red scarf, so rich it could melt ice, I heard a gentle paper like flutter. I swooped down to pick it up but noticed it was in another language. After work I had it scanned on the computers in the local library and the result was one of a life changing moment. A page had fallen out of a diary belonging to a sixteen-year-old Chinese girl and I had found it. Me. What are the odds? I read it. I did. And I saw the unexplainable differences that exist between her life and mine.

So Mr. President, I hope you can see them too. Childhood should BE just that. And we as children should be in a place where we can BE children. "I am a human being, not a human doing." Let's WORK against child labour, Mr. President, not alongside it.

Susan.

# David O'Keeffe
*Ireland, Age 16*

## Subject: CHILD LABOUR

My name is Pol. I am writing this letter in the hope that you, the leader of the free world, will be able to help us. I work in a factory along with a hundred other boys and girls, all aged between four and fifteen years old. They employ us because it is cheaper, because once you become an adult, you are too expensive for them to take responsibility for. I am the only one providing money for my family, so I must work hard.

How often must we plead until our cries are heard?! How often must we be exploited and beaten to within an inch of our sanity, before the world will listen to us?! My home is a shack in a shanty town of Southern Thailand. The children are starving, and must slave for hours upon hours to scrape out a miserable living for ourselves. We have experienced more pain, more trauma than anyone should have to face. We have always cried out for help, for comfort, and neither has ever come to us. I am pleading to you that we may live without slavery, may have fairer living conditions and, most of all, I just want a happy, safe childhood. Is that too much to ask? I speak for all the children who work in these conditions around the world, the children who suffer from the same fear and degradation that no human being should ever have to face.

Please, end child labour and slavery for all children. Shut down these factories, make us free from the pain and suffering that we have endured for so long; the same pain that has kept us awake every night in fear, searching for that ray of light in the dark room of our minds.

I'm sorry for having distracted you for so long with my letter, Mr. Obama, but I am so grateful to you that you took some time out of your presidential duties to read just one letter, a letter that contains the plight of a young boy who is echoing the thoughts of millions of other children around the world.

Thank you so, so much. I know you will do all you can to help us, and that your decisions will change our world for the better. I know it will take time, but we will wait for you with hope.

Maybe then, this hell will end.

Yours Sincerely,
Pol Chulanont

---

# Leia Valenzuela
## *United States, Age 16*

### Subject: CLIMATE CHANGE

---

"Are there any tissues in the car?!" Every morning is a routine for my sister and her nose. Unlike me, Molly is very sensitive to climate changes because of her allergies. It wasn't always like this though; until sixteen months ago, her allergies came and went, but more recently each day is a challenge. Due to the fact that "Monday we're expecting sunshine and Tuesday it's going to rain," says the weatherman, Molly can't rely on nature anymore. Despite her asthma, she also has trouble breathing when she wakes up with a runny nose and itchy eyes. Hearing about other people with allergies never really affected me until my family and I began experiencing the same thing with my sister. Not only is she affected by global warming, but my whole family has to watch her when she has trouble breathing and it kills us knowing that we – humans as a whole who are practically committing suicide – are the cause of it.

I have promised myself that I will do anything to help my sister – even though I know the truth about the earth and how humans are literally digging their own graves by smoking, throwing massive amounts of trash into landfills, failing to get smog checks, not using clean exhaust, wasting water, wasting electricity, killing and making animals extinct, and doing the hundreds of other wrongs that we humans have committed in our lifetimes.

I have not written this letter to rant on global warming, nor do I wish to bore you with five pages of nonsense. To be honest with you, Mr. President, the only reason I decided to write you this letter is because my Social Justice teacher said we would each get 15 points for simply writing you a letter and entering this competition. My teacher is a huge fan of yours and he definitely believes in you, and so do I.

I don't mean to put even more pressure on your job, but I would just like to say that I will be voting at the next election in four years, so if you want some brownie points, now is the time – not necessarily to prove yourself, but to be that one leader who stands out above the others; the one who made the right decision and didn't leave his/her nation in regret. Once I started this letter, it became more than an extra credit project; it turned into the impact that my voice, however small, can make a difference. If I'm lucky, I might even get the honor of you reading what I have to say. Every opinion counts, so whether it is my letter that you read or someone else's across the nation, you will know that we truly do care about our world and want to do whatever we can to delay the effects of global warming, as a united people.

# Jackie Lara

## *United States, Age 16*

### Subject: CHILD LABOUR

My mother always told me, "The most important thing to do is to get the best education I can possibly get because it will pay off in the future". When I think about child labor, I become angry and frustrated that these children do not have a chance to prove that they can become successful and get a high-quality job when they're older rather than having to break their backs when their little. So many children work every single day and are helpless and cannot change any of it. They're too small to be able to change drastic decisions about what they can do with their own life. They need an education to lead them to the right pathway of achievements and success. Right now, they have one choice: work, work, and work some more. However, with your help, they can have two choices: work their butts off, or go to school and become knowledgeable and be whatever they want to be such as a doctor, nurse, fireman, police officer, and maybe even becoming president.

# Rebecca Keating

*Ireland, Age 17*

## Subject: CLIMATE CHANGE

To put it simply, I am worried about our world – our future. We can not negotiate the facts. We can not negotiate the truth about the situation. The word of climate change is now roared in every corner of our globe. We see desertification, famine, rising sea levels. The warnings of climate change are shouting over our guzzling culture and we need to listen. I want to see a cleaner earth. I want our environment to be safe. This is my world, your world, our world, the world of future generations. This is our responsibility, our challenge, our obligation. I believe in us and our power to change.

As you said, we are the ones we have been waiting for.

Climate change is like a supertanker: it is very hard to slow it down once the engine is running. On the day-to-day timescale that humans normally deal with, climate change appears to be a slow process that takes place over decades and centuries. This generates a common misconception: if things get really bad, we can quickly change our behaviour and set it all right again. This is a fallacy. Dare I say it, a false hope. The climate responds slowly because it has an in-built resistance to change – which is why 200 years of vast fossil-fuel emissions have taken so long to produce an effect, and why any delay now in curbing carbon dioxide emissions will only store up bigger problems for the future. But they also know that the longer we continue to emit carbon dioxide, the longer it will take to alter the course of the climate supertanker – and the worse it will be for our children and grandchildren.

Mr. President, you once spoke of the moon being our new frontier. That we are one people, one nation. I ask you to stretch these metaphors when dealing with the issue of climate change in the developing world; less rain, spreading deserts, risks to food supplies, more storms and floods, and an increase in infectious diseases like malaria and dengue fever.

There is a massive vacancy for a world leader in the fight to preserve the atmosphere and the habitability of the earth; many people in many countries are fervently hoping that you, the 44th president, is the man who is willing and able to fill it. War and recession, tragically familiar sources of human misery, dominated. Yet it was what was missing from them that provoked my unwelcome thought. Terrible though they are, war and recession pass. Climate change is for ever. And the harder climate change bites, the likelier it is that profound and possibly irreversible changes will occur.

We must blaze the trail towards a future where we work together to combat climate change. It is not one man's responsibility but rather every citizen of this world and I say, yes we can.

# Kenny Adeyima
*Ireland, Age 16*

### Subject: CHILD LABOUR

I find it difficult to comprehend that in this age of ever-changing and evolving technology, children as young as three-years-old are braving hazardous conditions working long hours in sweatshops, plantations or on the streets of various cities in countries such as India and Kenya. Our breakthroughs in science and technology are tarnished by the ongoing child labour industry which puts millions of children's lives at risk every day. I recognise the work of organisations such as Concern and the International Labour Organisation (ILO) which runs the International Programme on the Elimination of Child Labour (IPEC). The work done by these bodies and their volunteers is creating opportunities for progress and improvements in the lives of many children around the world. However, so much more needs to be done.

I believe also that too much of the population remain blind to the crisis of child labour as not enough awareness is created and a lot of people don't see it as their concern because it doesn't affect their day-to-day lives. You said in your inaugural address, "What is required of us now is a new era of responsibility"; this is a global issue although it doesn't affect everyone in the same manner. I'd like to give you a deeper look by sharing the stories of one young Indian boy who was unchained from the difficult and uncertain future of child workers in India.

My name is Shreyas Kaj; I am a 15-year-old student now attending secondary school in Mumbai, India. I am very grateful and fortunate to be given the opportunity to get an education especially as so many other kids that are in the same situation as I was are still trapped and can't see any hope for a better future. I was five-years-old when I was taken off the street while rummaging through heaps of rubbish and brought to the factory. I was overwhelmed at first as I was given food by strangers who seemed genuinely prepared to help me – an orphan off the street. I quickly realised, however, that I would have preferred life outside the walls of the factory to what I faced as a child labourer ...

# Emily Rutherford

*Ireland, Age 17*

**Subject: CLIMATE CHANGE**

Dear President Obama,

I speak to you across the seas, as one dreamer to another. I have little time in this world, and maybe I am foolish to hope that you would help us. But there are not many we can turn to now.

I have never been to your land ... now that I am old and sick I never will. It is many years away, 7,000 miles, so they say. But I have heard the young people talk of you. And I have heard you speak on the radio. Though we do not speak the same language, you and I, there is something in your voice which I recognise, which I have not heard in many years.

This is Tuvalu: we are a tiny island, far smaller than any of your great lands. Our children are sick and our language dying. The oceans are emptied by boats as long as the beach, the metal monsters devour the forests. And slowly, quietly, the sea creeps up on us.

I am an old woman, and so I remember a time when it was not like this. Many seasons ago, our forests were lush and bountiful, full of flowers and medicines and plants that have disappeared forever. The island was green and living. Now it shrivels up and dies during the dry season to brown cooking tinder, and we gaze at the sky and beg for rain.

This is not new in my many years. But it is worse and worse during the years of my daughter's daughter. It is she that writes this letter for me. The young people leave the island and learn to speak another tongue. There is nothing for them here.

And all the time, the sea continues to rise.

I talk to my daughter's daughter, I open my eyes to what is happening, and I weep for what has befallen us. She says it is your people who have caused our problem, but how can you control the sea?

She says to me that your nation is burning up the world, to power your big cars and televisions and factories. You have cleared the forests to make a place for your cattle. My daughter's daughter tells me that your people have so much to eat it becomes a problem.

How can this be? It took me a long time to understand how anyone could have too much food.

And while I am struggling to understand, the sea continues to rise. The sea is our life, yes, but also our enemy. It is how we survive, the source of our food, yet it threatens our survival. It is the first sound we hear at dawn and the last at sundown: the soft whisper of the tides on the sand and the crash of the waves on the rocks.

They say you are the one who will change things, you who have the same colour skin as me. I want to believe this, but I am an old woman and I know promises are broken more often than they are kept.

# Mary Anne Lambert

*Ireland, Age 17*

**Subject: CHILD LABOUR**

I invite you now to travel back in time with me to 1832, England. Early on a cold, dark morning, a five-year-old girl is forced down a Yorkshire coalmine. She has to work in the uncomfortable conditions for twelve hours a day. Her job is to open and close the trapdoors for miners. She is paid little more than the equivalent of 2c for her twelve hour day. When asked about her job, she honestly but haltingly replies, "It does not tire me, but I have to trap without a light ... and I'm scared ... I never go to sleep". Sarah, like thousands of other children, was exposed to seriously harmful conditions and denied the joy and freedom of childhood. In later life her back became deformed from a lifetime of crouching and bending. Her eyesight was damaged from working in a damp, poorly lit environment. She was denied formal education and died illiterate. Like many others, Sarah did not reach the age of thirty.

I would like to tell you, Mr President, that child labour as I have just described it, is history. It appears to belong to the Dark Ages. Sadly, it is not history. Child labour is very much part of today's world. Let me invite you to Peru, 2009. Rebecca, a seven-year-old girl, dresses as a boy in order to wash cars with her older brother in the streets. She works 10 hours a day for $1.50. Across the globe in Nepal, a five-year-old boy, Bhagi, begins work as a domestic labourer in the house of his father's employer. He takes the cows to graze, cuts grass, cleans utensils and does other housework from early in the morning until late at night. He knows nothing of childhood as you and I, the children of the West, experienced it – nothing of leisure, sports, school...

International legislation and convention seeking to end child labour have not been enforced. The time has come to take action. The General Secretary of the UN, Ban Ki-moon, stated: "The world wants no new promises." Instead, what is needed are finances and political will. Some governments and businesses see child labour as a way to compete internationally as it keeps costs and prices low. These corrupt governments need to be addressed. If necessary, a boycott of countries where child labour is practised should be put in place. Existing legislation must be enforced or child labour will continue.

As a father yourself, President Obama, I am sure you wish your children to enjoy the full extent of their childhood. Indeed, I imagine you would do all you could to prevent your two young daughters having to work. Now in your new position, I set you this challenge. Now is the time for you to do all you can to prevent the children of the world having to work. You have the power to effect incredible change in the world. In your inauguration speech you referred to the "God given promise that all are equal, all are free and all deserve a chance to pursue their full measure of happiness". Fix your eyes now on the children of the world and free them from the slavery of child labour. Make the abolition of child labour your new horizon and let America lead the world once more.

Can you take on this task Mr. Obama? Yes you can!

# Suzanne Ni Fhionnain

*Ireland, Age 16*

## Subject: WORLD HUNGER

Mr. Obama, what is the reason for fifteen million children dying of hunger each year?

We often talk about our quality of life or our standard of living while in the third world countries the focus is towards the mere sustaining of life. Every 3.6 seconds someone dies of hunger! How can we, at a time when people are not getting enough to eat, live a life far beyond what many could even imagine? At least eighty per cent of humanity lives on less than ten dollars a day, while the assets of the world's three richest men are more than the combined GNP of all the least developed countries on the planet.

World agriculture produces enough food to provide everyone in the world with at least 2,720 kilocalories per person daily, far more than what half the world will receive today. The principal problem is that many people do not have sufficient land to grow or income to purchase enough food. Why? The imbalanced distribution of money. The poorest forty per cent of the world's population accounts of five per cent of global income, while the richest twenty per cent account for three-quarters of the world income. It currently costs thirty times as much, in terms of energy and resources to feed a North American as it does to feed a Pakistani.

Although Pakistan produces wheat, rice and fruits such as strawberries, mangos and melons, the heavy export taxes and trade barriers set by wealthy countries make it difficult for them to benefit from this.

The indifference of individuals and their governments is one of the main reasons why 183 million children weigh less than they should, or why one in six elderly people have an inadequate diet. It really is the innocent who suffer in our world today. So the next time we take a trip to London, Paris or New York, we should think of the 500 million Asian, African or Latin Americans who are living in what the World Bank has described as "absolute poverty". We should recognise the significant strain our standard of living places on the world's economy.

The world community has both the knowledge and the resources to eliminate hunger. Doing this requires us to ground our choices for the common good. Right now, this is not happening. To satisfy the world's sanitation and food requirements would cost only 13 billion dollars – what the people of the European Union and United States of America spend on perfume each year. We must not only consider what we should do to feed the hungry but we must also consider what we should do to limit our indulgent lifestyles. Because, as Martin Luther King once said:

*Before you eat your breakfast this morning, you have de-
pended on half the world, this is the way our world is struc-
tured. We will not have not have peace on earth until we
recognise this basic fact.*

Mr. Obama, these people depend on you, on me, on us. Let us
help them.

Yours in hope.

---

# Carla Sunderman
*Ireland, Age 18*

## Subject: CLIMATE CHANGE

---

Africa is your ancestral home. Unfortunately, it is also the most
vulnerable to the effects of climate change due its defencelessness
owing to its dependence on rain-fed agriculture. There have been
increases in severe droughts and food shortages as a result.
Worldwide, the annual number of reported droughts has increased more than three-fold since the 1970s. The cost of clean energy is beyond what most African countries can afford. The responsibility falls upon the richer developed nations of the world
who use the most energy anyway.

By lessening climate change, you will not only be saving the
planet, but will lessen world hunger, poverty, mass deaths due to
floods, droughts, hurricanes, heat waves and other extreme
weather conditions directly linked with climate change. You will
be saving not only the lives of humans, but also of this planet's

unique animals and wildlife and the planet's trees and plants, all of which are massively important to our survival on earth.

The following excerpt of one of your speeches is probably one of the best examples of what your nation now needs to follow through with:

> *"We will make it clear to the world that America is ready to lead. To protect our climate and our collective security, we must call together a truly global coalition."*

# Tammy Oruwariye
*United States, Age 16*

## Subject: WORLD HUNGER

Ever since I was a little girl, I always wanted to help the poor. Growing up from a Nigerian background, I was taught by my grandparents to treat others with respect and help those in need. Whenever I go to Nigeria, I always try to give the little I have to those begging on the streets. I often used to cry at the mere sight of an emaciated child begging for food to eat. In 2004, I was schooling in Nigeria. I participated in a community service club that helped increase my awareness of poverty. Within that club, we frequently made trips to the local orphanage. In one of our visits to the orphanage, I helped feed at least five babies. I overheard the owner of the orphanage complaining about the lack of money to provide for the babies in the orphanage. Hence, there was a shortage of food and milk to give to these orphans. It was there that I realised world hunger is a growing problem around the world. Both hunger and malnutrition account for over nine million deaths each year worldwide. The truth is that about five million of these deaths are children. Hunger and malnutrition are one of the leading causes of child mortalities. In order to protect our future, we must find a solution to this growing problem.

# Jacklyn Nagle
*Ireland, Age 18*

**Subject:** CHILD LABOUR

As you read this letter I would ask you to keep your own two daughters, Malia and Sasha in mind – their carefree natures, their happy smiles, their innocent wish for a puppy. In a letter to them you described how you wanted them "to grow up in a world with no limits on your dreams and no achievements beyond your reach, and to grow into compassionate, committed women who will help build that world. And [you] want every child to have the same chances to learn and dream and grow and thrive". I want to draw your attention to over 200 million children who are denied this childhood, this development and these dreams; as one in every seven children worldwide is involved in child labour. The plight of these children is being ignored and as a result child labour is reaching epidemic proportions. I am calling on you, Mr President, to fight for these forgotten ones, as to quote Mohandas Gandhi, "Be the change that you want to see in the world".

There are many forms of exploitation in the world, many kinds of injustice and violence. But child labour is exploitation, injustice and violence rolled into one. This year is the 20th anniversary of the UN declaration of the rights of the child and many international labour laws exist to protect children. Why then, are so many children subject to exploitation?

So, how can we tackle this problem? Education is the key to success! Ensuring that all children go to school and receive good quality education is really the only way to remove these children from full-time work.

Through education the plight of child labourers will be alleviated. Incentives need to be provided for poor parents to send their children to school. One solution is to replace child workers with their parents (who may be unemployed) and this may actually increase the family's income because adults are more highly paid.

To quote Lord Byron, "Words are things, and a small drop of ink, falling like dew, upon a thought, produces that which makes thousands, perhaps millions, think." I'm beseeching you, Mr President, to use your voice, your words and your power to ensure a brighter future for these children. We know that we have the means, the ability and the capacity to eliminate child labour. We need the will! We must demand this day and night. We must let our cry of protest be heard. We owe it to the children of this world to amplify their voices!

# Brendan O'Gara
*Ireland, Age 16*

**Subject: CLIMATE CHANGE**

Scientists tell us that there is still time to help make a turnaround. If we cut down our carbon footprint, then it is possible for the ozone layer to be repaired fully. On the other hand, if we continue the way we are going, then we as a human race may not even exist in 100 years' time. This is a very frightening prospect that should spark people into action. Already people are being killed due to the sensational force of Mother Nature. You can provide the leadership to help us get through this epidemic. It is the greatest challenge facing us today.

... It is a problem that everyone is talking about. I am concerned about the well being of countries in the developing world. We need to help the countries that find it difficult to help themselves. I have great faith in you as a leader. You certainly have become president at a difficult time. Yet, when the going gets tough, the tough get going. The poorest people in the world have endured terrible hardship and this has to stop now! If we work together then we can turn the tide somewhat. I want to wish you every possible success in the future and thank you for taking the time to read this letter.

# Louise McAteer

*Ireland, Age 16*

## Subject: CLIMATE CHANGE

When we in the First World think of global warming and related issues, we tend to think of the superficial problems it will cause, e.g. "Well, that's my skiing holiday gone out the window then", or "Petrol prices are going up *again*?? We often forget that the people who will really suffer from our mistakes will be the people in the developing world.

Sir, even as we speak, desertification is worsening in the Sahel region of Africa. In Mali, crops are withering, animals are dying and people are fleeing before the indefatigable advances of the suffocating sand. Desertification causes mass migration from the affected area and this causes huge problems of overcrowding in the countries where the displaced people settle.

We in the First World must also help developing countries to *make their own contributions to the task of combating climate change.* We can do this by educating people in these nations about environmental issues, sharing some of our technological knowledge with them, and giving them financial aid so that they can work with us for the common good. Remember, Mr. President, it is not just the developing world who are in a vulnerable situation; if global warming continues unchecked, then we will *all* have to face the consequences.

One of your most famous predecessors, George Washington, reputedly said, "I cannot tell a lie". Well, now the world is relying on you, Sir, to continue the tradition of fighting for the truth – however inconvenient the truth may be. I sincerely hope that you appreciate the importance of this issue, Mr President, and that you will use your influence and persuasive skills to make change happen. I wish you the very best of luck in your future efforts to combat the terrible effects of climate change on the developing world in particular and the world in general. Thank you, Sir, for taking time to read my letter.

# Lindsay Merryman

*United States, Age 16*

### Subject: WORLD HUNGER

I lie on the floor, thinking to myself in a voice without language. The world seems so strange to me sideways. I feel I should start sliding any moment as if I were lying on a hill. The sound of my breathing startles me. The rasping is like wind through the tall grass. Perhaps wind is breath, the breath of a million people, people sighing and hurting, and hungry. My mother is crying in the corner behind me, but I do not hear her anymore, only feel her shaking through the floor. There are four other children in this hut. Some are crying. I don't hear them either. Something inside me says they are my brothers and my sisters, that I should comfort them, being the oldest, the man of the family. I am young though, only nine or ten, maybe a little older. I have memorised the creases in the walls by now, having traced them in my mind a thousand times. When I close my eyes, I see those faint black lines on my eyelids. I fear for a moment they are traced into my eyes, but they quickly leave me. No, mother is rocking back and forth. I look back at her and she is rubbing her breasts and sobbing. She is trying to make her milk flow again, but it is not working. She realised last night that her milk had stopped from not eating. The baby will surely die because it is too young to eat anything else. That baby, lying there next to Mother in a dirty blanket, that baby will never have a name. Only children who live to five years old receive a name. Only me and one other child in this room has a name, the two other children are still too young and at least one of the will have to die. And mother will say which one. There is only enough food now for her, me, and the girl Janna. The youngest will die. I drift off into sleep, fearing the whole time that I may never wake up. Will death be like sleeping? Like one moment you are awake and then you just aren't anymore? Do you wake up somewhere else or just never wake up?

My name is Kadiri and I am a boy in Africa. And I am dying of hunger.

# Emma Verschoyle

*Ireland, Age 16*

## Subject: CLIMATE CHANGE

I would like to thank you sincerely for reading my letter. I'm just a normal girl but I have a big dream and I know it can come true. This may be a cliché but it is the truth. I may not be able to write speeches like you or speak to crowds like you but I am trying and if I can make a difference in even one person's life I will be happy, and if I can make you think about what I have said then I will be extremely happy. You can't stop progress but you can speed it up! There are so many problems in the world and if we sort this one out now then it will be one less problem to worry about and we can concentrate on other problems (which you will hopefully be receiving a letter from me on too).

I will not give up on this and I know that you won't either which is the reason I wrote to you before even thinking of writing to anyone else.

Thank you for the time that you took away from your busy schedule and don't forget to turn off the stand-by lights in your house!

# Andrea Romani

## *United States, Age 17*

### Subject: WORLD HUNGER

We all talk about making that special difference, but do we actually try and act? No, many of us do not so I want to be that difference. I want to be able to inspire others so that they can care and share the love with the less fortunate. They need food, we should feed them with what we can. I am not talking about a whole buffet but I am talking about a small meal. They will be happy with just that, I know it. We can not just wait around and see for all the problems of the world to go away because I know that it is not possible, but actions can help. With everyone working together, we can help and that would be all that they need. They need to see that there are people in the world that want to help and want to be kind and caring. We need to show them that we want to do this, not because we are obligated but from the bottom of our hearts. Hunger is an important issue in today's society and I hope that we can all really make this difference even if we have to start from scratch. I would want to see this done for the goodness of all and, with time, we will see that difference and what we did to save other people's lives.

# Qiu Meng Fogarty

*United States, Age 16*

### Subject: CHILD LABOUR

Mudiwa runs into the shanty and the woman wipes her tears so that the child won't see her mother cry. Mudiwa clambers on to her mother's lap and sits there smiling, innocent and adorable, oblivious to the mood of the conversation. Unable to think of what to say, you crouch silently in the poor shanty for several minutes. The woman takes her calloused hands and wraps them around your smooth hand. You realise that you are now the one crying, moved by the woman's story and her profound strength. You want to know what you can do, but how can one person make such a difference?

"Tell my story," the woman smiles, looking deep into your eyes, "tell my story."

# Ruth Keating

*Ireland, Age 17*

## Subject: CHILD LABOUR

Child labour is an insult to humanity. It is unjust and cruel. Children are enslaved, exploited, isolated in domestic work, toil in mines and work in unimaginable squalor. We are damaging and crippling our future for the sake of now. Child labour is not child work. Child labour is the time bomb lodged against the heart of liberty.

Of course, people will say that it is all for the sake of the future, but what if the "future" still hasn't arrived in thirty, forty or even fifty years' time? Four or eight years from now you will be more disappointed by the things that you didn't do than by the things that you did. I believe in the power of democracy and I do not want to, nor do I, doubt hope. It is the responsibility of anybody who values the price of human dignity to stand up and face this most monumental of challenges and this gross insult to human dignity. I pray that words of hope shall be whispered by slaves and abolitionists as they and we blaze a new trail towards freedom and that your words of hope shall be believed and felt by the forgotten children world over, and that you will say to these children yes we can, yes we can.

It is somebody exactly like you, with your notoriety and idealistic, but realistic nature, who has the power to write out the stamp of inequality on the world, a place where all things should be possible. Education is the key to ending the exploitation of children. Every child, every citizen, every individual needs to be inspired to achieve their human potential. Because it is on this, that history will judge us. The importance of education as a route to freedom is one that cannot be underestimated. Ending poverty and increasing access to education are crucial tools in the fight against child labour.

"If there is anyone out there who still doubts that America is a place where all things are possible, who still questions the power of our democracy, tonight is your answer."

As these are your words I beg you to fulfil the promise that lies in them, not just for all Americans but for all citizens of the world, all citizens seeking change. Let these children feel the blaze of undying hope and the promise that lies in all humanity. Let them know that all men are created equal. Let them know that they too are entitled to life, liberty and the pursuit of happiness. If you give somebody the opportunity of freedom they can make their own emancipation.

We are one people, we are one nation, we are one world. With your help we can abolish child labour and spread emancipation to all children of the world.

# Roisin Guihen

*Ireland, Age 17*

### Subject: WORLD HUNGER

A hate-spreading monster is taking over the world we share, Mr. President. He has crept in silently and captured and imprisoned our beautiful dove of peace. He preys on the poverty stricken and prides himself on producing pain. He is the devil's sidekick sent to the earth dressed as hunger. Rapidly he is fulfilling the word of the devil. Mr. Obama, the wise people of America have handed you the keys to the White House. Connected to these keys are the keys to change. You now hold the power to initiate change in our world. With this power comes a heavy burden caused predominantly by the works of this demon. Together, we must work to lighten this load. We must lift off the miseries laid down by hunger. We must demolish his disasters. As a symbol of hope, change, of possibility, it is to you we must turn to help end the reign of this cataclysmic force. Together we can free the dove of peace.

Hunger has no mercy. It destroys the lives not merely of men and women, it particularly enjoys preying on our most vulnerable – our children. It starts inside and way below their throats slowly, slowly creeping upwards. It draws back down as they inhale then pulls itself up yet again. It flashes light but not in a visible sense. It hurts, no it warns. Warns and threatens, all the while grabbing at the insides of their little bodies and pulling itself upwards until it gets an answer: food, an answer that in many mouths never comes. Fifteen million children die of hunger each year. One in twelve people internationally is malnourished, including 160 million children under the age of five. Malnutrition is implicated in more than 50% of child deaths worldwide, a proportion unmatched by any infectious disease since the Black Death. Every 3.6 seconds hunger murders.

Hunger is sharper then the sword. If we are going to end wars on this earth we are going to have to make the war on hunger our number one priority. Hunger prides itself on making a thief of any man. A hungry man cannot see right or wrong, he just sees food. It is hunger who persuades people to violence. Starvation, not sin, is the parent of modern crime. Hunger is insolent, Mr. President, it will be fed. Let you, however, not war, be the one to feed it.

The people in your world are hungry, Mr. President. I am hungry, hungry for change. I am hungry for an end to the dying and a start to the living, an end to the hunger and a start to the peace. It is you we have chosen to lead us. It is you who must feed us. End hunger's crusade. Turn those keys to change. Let the dove of peace fly.

# Part Three

# ADULT CATEGORY

## (over 19 years old)

THE WHITE HOUSE
Office of the Press Secretary

FOR IMMEDIATE RELEASE June 12, 2009

## Statement by President Barack Obama on
## World Day Against Child Labor

Even in this modern era, children around the world are forced to work in deplorable and often dangerous conditions at a time in their lives when they should be in classrooms and playgrounds. Global child labor perpetuates a cycle of poverty that prevents families and nations from reaching their full potential. That's why, earlier this week, Secretary of Labor Hilda Solis reaffirmed my Administration's commitment to this issue by announcing $60 million to fight child labor.

I also find it fitting that this year's World Day Against Child Labor focuses on drawing attention to the particular plight young girls face. Of the 218 million child laborers worldwide, 100 million are girls – more than half of whom are exposed to hazardous work. That's unacceptable, and this world cannot allow it. We must stand united in opposition to child labor and recommit ourselves to ending this practice in all its forms – today and every day.

# 1st Place – Adult

## Ndifor Eleves Funnui
*Niger*

**Subject: World Hunger**

Dear President Obama,

You cannot imagine how excited I was on the 20th of January 2009 when you took the oath of office as the first Afro-American to rule the United States of America. Mr. President, your roots are spread right up to the developing world and I am hopeful that you shall be of great help in the fight against world hunger, especially in developing countries. I am equally aware of the fact that you are a very busy man but if you do not mind, I would like to share the plight of children in developing countries that are facing hunger every minute of their life.

Mr. President, like many children in developing countries, I live in a family with many members going from direct brothers and sisters, half-brother and sisters, cousins, uncles and aunts. Hunger has always been our companion. Given the family size, it is impossible for those in charge of bringing food to our table to make ends meet because there are too many mouths to feed. I have discovered that family planning is one of the major causes of hunger in developing countries and unless something is done to cut down birth rate in these countries, their populations shall continue to live in hunger. Sir, I propose that your administration helps developing countries to cut down their birth rate. This can be done through the United Nations Population Agency by giving this Agency enough funds to promote reproductive health in developing countries. If parents can limit the number of mouths they have to feed, this will greatly help in chasing away hunger from the world.

Sir, my mother has eight children (five girls and three boys) and I am the first child. At the age of 28, I now have five nieces and nephews. I know you will smile and ask yourself how this can be. It is simple; our father was obliged to withdraw my sisters from school and marry them away because he could no more cope with the feeding his numerous wives and children. This is the same fate that awaits girls in many developing countries. They are always the first victims of hunger. I was so shocked to see my sisters getting married before the age of fifteen. Sir, take a look at Malia and Sasha and imagine being obliged to marry them away at the age of twelve in order to use their bride price to feed other members of the family. Can you imagine yourself doing that? I know the answer is NO but that is the daily experience in some parts of the world as a result of hunger. For us boys, we are sent to work in people's farms, building sites and, worst still, to beg or steal. Hunger has transformed our countries into a jungle where people do what they can to survive.

Mr. President, our farmlands are disappearing; in some countries like my dear Niger, the Sahara Desert has covered a good part our farmlands and in other countries, farmlands have been transformed into residential areas because of their population boom and for other countries, seawaters are wiping out farmlands. The worst of it all is that the remaining lands we have are not fertile enough to produce enough food to feed us. It is for this reason that I would like your administration to look at ways of helping the agricultural system of developing countries. Sir, we need to be capacity-built on modern agricultural techniques as well as be given modern farming tools and seeds. Unless the agricultural systems in developing countries are modernised, the populations shall never be able to produce enough food to feed themselves. Diversified and modernised agricultural techniques remain one of the best solutions to combat world hunger.

Sir, in recent months, things have become worse as concerns food prices. Given that our lands cannot provide enough food to feed us, we are obliged to import food but this is becoming almost impossible given the recent increase in food prices. I do not know how you can help reduce food prices but I know that it is one of the main underlying causes of hunger in developing countries, and I also know that you have many economic experts in your administration that can help look at means of reducing food prices. There is no need having food in the market when the population cannot afford for it. To me, this is the same thing like asking a hungry child to sit in front of the television set and watch people eating.

For the past decades, developed countries have been spending a lot of money on developing yet the situation has not improved and to speak the truth, it shall never improve. Ask me why. Western governments have been making a lot of mistakes by giving aid to developing countries through their governments and most of the time with no follow-up measures. Sir, most of the money developed countries send to help developing countries end up in bank accounts in the countries from which the money came. Our governments are so corrupt that they do not mind selling their mothers to have money. I know governments that will sell a mirror to a blind man. Corruption remains one of the major pillars on which hunger still leans in developing countries. Food and financial aid never reach the vulnerable populations. You must have heard that when my country was in the middle of a food crisis in 2005, trucks loaded with tons of food from the World Food Programme destined for my country were intercepted heading to neighbouring countries like Nigeria, Ghana and Benin to be sold. I am sure you shall not ask me who planned such a devilish act. If you do decide to help in the fight against hunger, you should do so through international or national Non-Governmental Organisations because they always have the love of the population at heart.

I read from somewhere that your administration was very interested in fighting terrorism and HIV/AIDS. If I am not mistaken, this is not a new thing given that other presidents before you had the same objectives but they never succeeded. Sir, I know there are many great experts around you that can better advise you but let me tell you something that can help you fight HIV/AIDS and terrorism. If you invest on the fight against world hunger, you shall greatly succeed in HIV/AIDS and terrorism. It might sound foolish but Sir, know that because of hunger, children leave school and end up on the streets where they become vulnerable and are manipulated. Girls become prostitutes and have unprotected sex so as to survive. There are many girls that have sex in exchange for food. We all know the relationship between unprotected sex and HIV/AIDS. When these children are hungry and vulnerable, terrorist groups easily manipulate and send them on suicide missions. This is why I am asking you to first of all fight hunger if you want to fight HIV/AIDS and terrorism. Think of how many bags of rice, flour or millet the cost of a bomb falling in Iraq can buy and you shall discover that it is cheaper to fight hunger than to fight terrorism.

Mr President, as many children go hungry and abandon school so as to work in order to feed their families, the future of developing countries remains bleak because these children suffer for life when they are being malnourished in their childhood. Youths in developing countries have understood that their countries have no future for them and this explains why many of them die trying to cross into Europe. Sir, I am sure you know that fighting hunger is some sort of investment because money used in solving problems resulting from hunger could be invested in other sectors of the economy.

Mr. President, I will end here but before I do so, I would like to plead with you to look at Malia and Sasha in their eyes and tell me if you would like to see them in the situation in which children in developing countries find themselves. If your answer is no, then do something to fight world hunger.

Yours sincerely,

Ndifor Eleves Funui
Republic of Niger

# SECOND PLACE – ADULT

## Cathy Howlett
*Ireland*

**Subject: CHILD LABOUR**

Dear President Obama,

My name is Niamh. I am seven. I'm in Ms. O'Reilly's class in school. She's nice because she lets us do colouring. Are you a wizard? My Daddy says that you're going to change the world so I think you must be a wizard. Do you have a magic wand? I think it's ok if you don't cos I saw a film where a little girl with red shoes goes to see a wizard somewhere and he's able to do magic and send her to another place and he doesn't even have a magic wand, he's just very clever. I know that you're very clever cos you use a lot of big words when you're speaking on the telly. If you're a wizard and your very clever does that mean that you're able to send me somewhere else like the wizard in that film? I don't want to live in Ireland anymore. I want to go and live with my friend Nana. She lives in Injia. She used to live here in Ireland but the man who is in charge of Ireland told Nana's Daddy that he couldn't live here anymore and that he had to go home. I think its cos there's no jobs for Injian Daddies. My Daddy says that there's a session on and that the whole world is sad. Nana was sad cos she had to leave Ms. O Reilly's class before we got to learn our 7 times tables. Nana is my best friend; she sat with me at the green table. She is very good at colouring. She's smaller than me cos she's only six. My Mammy

174

was very sad when Nana's Mammy told her she was going home. Nana's Mammy works in a factory. She told my Mammy about it and my Mammy doesn't want her to go back. But I think it's nice. Nana's Mammy makes clothes for Irish Mammies and works with a lot of other Injian Mammies. Nana told me that when she goes back she won't have to go to school anymore. She is allowed to go to work making clothes in the factory where her Mammy works. She is so lucky cos she doesn't have to learn her multiplication tables. She gets to go to the factory all day long with other boys and girls. Nana's sister goes to the factory everyday too. She is ten but she didn't come to Ireland. She stayed in Injia with her Granny. Nana told me all about the big factory where she will work. All the Mammies work upstairs making the nice clothes. The boys and girls like Nana and her sister sit downstairs. They put the buttons on the nice clothes then give them to the man who sends them to Ireland. They are very 'spensive clothes so the Mammies who make them must be very rich. Nana's sister gets 10p for everyday she works. She is lucky cos my favourite sweets are liquorice laces and they cost 20p in the shops. Nana will be able to buy a lot of them when she gets money for putting the buttons on the nice clothes. I'm only allowed have liquorice laces on Fridays. I wish I was allowed to go to the factory with Nana instead of school. I don't like homework. Nana doesn't have to do homework cos she gets to go to the factory instead of school. Nana and her sister are allowed to stay out really late too. She told me that they stay in the factory till night time. I'm not allowed stay up late, I have to go to bed after cartoons, before grown up telly comes on. Nana is really lucky that she gets to stay up until grown up telly comes on. I wonder if she watches it in the factory with the other children when they're finished making the nice clothes? I'm not allowed watch grown up telly cos I have to get up early for school. Nana says she gets up early too. There is no Superquinn in Injia so Nana and her Granny get up before the sun is shining to get food and water in the next village. I think the food and water is nicer there than in their own village cos they walk for a long time to get it. It's like the take-away my Daddy drives to. It's far away but my Daddy says it's nicer than the one that's near our house. Nana's Granny must like the water in the other village better too. Nana and her Granny have to walk before the sun comes up cos the sun is very hot in Injia. The sun is never hot in Ireland, its always raining and we can't go out to play. I think Nana and her friends go to the beach to play sandcastles on the days that they don't want to go and make the nice clothes in the factory. I would like to go and play sandcastles in Injia. When Nana comes back she eats her breakfast and then goes to the factory with her Mammy and her sister. She eats lots of rice. She must really like it cos she even eats it for her breakfast instead of Coco Pops. She says that sometimes it makes her sick cos it's dirty. I told her she should ask her Mammy to clean it with washing up liquid or else just ask for Pop Tarts instead. When Nana goes to the factory she has to go downstairs with the other boys and girls. She says there are loads and loads and loads of them. I wish I had that many people to play with. I only have 2 best friends. Nana has lots of friends in the factory. Nana says that it is very hot and very dark down there. I think the air conditioning is broken and the man has to fix it. Nana says that sometimes it is so dark that she can't even see the buttons on the clothes she is making. I told her that she should get one of the big boys or girls to turn on the light for her. Nana says that they have to be very quiet in the factory cos they are hiding. I think the man who owns the factory likes to play hide and seek and the boys and girls aren't allowed make any noise in case anyone outside the factory comes in and finds them. Nana is really good at hide and seek and she says that she never makes noise. One time when Nana's family was in Ireland they heard a story that a man and a woman came over from America and found all the boys and girls. They were very cross with the man who owned the factory. I think the game was over after that and the man had to go to jail cos he was no good at hide and seek. The man who owns the factory now isn't very good at it either. He never finds the boys and girls all day even though they hide in the same place all the time. None of the Mammies ever find them either and when it gets dark and its time to go home the boys and girls just come out and tell them where they were. I think people in Injia are really silly! When some of the boys and girls make noise the man is really cross and shouts at them. Sometimes he even gives them a smack. I think he just doesn't want to loose the game and go to jail like the other man did.

Mr. Obama, can you send me to Injia? I want to play with Nana and make nice clothes and buy lots of liquorice laces. I think I can show them how to play hide and seek properly and maybe I can even ask the man to fix the air conditioning so that Nana and the other boys and girls aren't too hot all the time. I don't want to learn my 7 times tables, I want to go over to Injia to see my best friend and play sandcastles when it's hot. I hope that you are really clever or else a wizard so that you can send me to Injia.

Lots of love,

Niamh xxxxx

# JOINT THIRD PLACE – ADULT

## Brian Harding
*Ireland*

**Subject: CLIMATE CHANGE**

Dear President Obama,

I am so so tired. Every day I am closer to death. The pressure is huge on me. My Family needs help. We need help because things have been getting tougher and tougher for us. We feel like we're letting everyone down. It is a withering feeling.

Our ancestors tell us through the winds of our humble beginnings in the central Americas, how humans who knew the land and the ecology of their surroundings, identified us, saw potential in us, bred us, and turned us into the maize that you know today. Today, I am found in a small field in the west of Kenya. Mr Obama, you will know it too for you claim ancestry here as well.

As maize, we have felt the increases of heat more intensely than others. As humans have debated whether 'their' world is getting warmer, we have suffered and our keepers have been trying to adapt. Farmers have grown maize in Africa for such a short time. But yet they are so reliant on us. In some places, we are the only food available. When the rains are good, we stand tall and farmers exclaim that they will have a good year. But it is so hard to stand tall now. The soil is so scorched, has lost its moisture and has become so hard. My roots struggle to push through.

I want the farmers to grow me alongside other plants. All life on this planet knows that diversity is strength and gives us all resilience. Why do you rely only on us? Why do you make yourself so vulnerable? My ears allow me to listen and hear extension workers in suits come and proclaim putting more fertilizers on the soil as the only solution. I hear my keeper say he can't afford such inputs, that things were too difficult last year, that if he had a different type of maize, life would be better or that if he had more land it would be easier. But the poor advice still comes. My keeper doesn't know about how the climate in changing. In fact, the only thing he cares about is his family. He is not selfish. He seems to be a good man.

I would like to be able to give him advice myself. I would like to be able to say that things are different now, that things have changed since his father tended this very same land. I would tell him that I am tired. I would tell him that the soil beneath is tired. I would tell him that we have taken so many of the minerals from the soil that it too needs help. It needs time to rest. I would tell him just as he rests when the sun is too hot; I too need shade and protection. I need more water, but I know there is less water. I hear him speaking of water more than he did in the past. There is less. I know there is less rain. I feel its loss the most. My leaves turn yellow and the farmer curses me. I have let him down. I feel I have let everyone down.

I want the farmer to listen to his wife. I hear her speak of the plants that she grows in her kitchen garden. They flourish. Yes, they are few but they grow strong. She tends them delicately. She swaps seeds and seedlings with her women friends who come by and drink Kenyan tea and tell stories of the village. She grows herbs and flavours soups and stews with them. But the farmer only cares about maize. All of his hopes and dreams are in us, in maize. We can't provide what he wants. We can't guarantee that every seedling that he plants will be strong, that we will even grow above knee height. He seems to make mistakes now. It embarrasses him. He seems to plant at the wrong times. He doesn't watch the seasons. The rainy season does not come when it should. The small rains didn't arrive last year. The dry season was interrupted by rains this year. The world is changing. I can't adapt and either can the farmer that keeps me. It seems to be changing too fast. Our vulnerability is everyone's vulnerability.

Last night, I heard the farmer and his wife speak of school fees. Their eldest son is 14 years old. He is a man now. They think he should go and work in Nairobi. They could afford the bus fare and he could stay with the farmer's sister who lives there in a place called Kibera. He could then send back money and they could afford more fertilizer. It would only be for a while they explain to their son. Maybe he could come back to school when the crop is better. But I know it could be forever, because nothing seems to be guaranteed anymore. They tell their son that someday he will inherit the land and it will be his when his parents pass away. But leaving the land means he will never understand the land, or me, or the soil, or the way that some insects lay their eggs on us, or what I am telling him when I turn yellow, or wilt a little, or lean over or even die. He will lose something that can only truly be learned by watching me grow. He will not be here to see when his father will eventually give up on me.

Oh, Mr. Obama, the world says you will listen to the voices of the disenfranchised. I am a voice that almost no one listens to anymore. Can you hear me? Come here and tell my keeper that I need his help. Tell him that I need to be nurtured in a different way. Tell my keeper to not send his son to the city. Tell him to find a way to keep him in school and get an education. Tell him that things need to change. Tell him that he needs to listen to his wife. Tell him that I am not the only solution to all his problems. Tell him to try something new. Tell him that he should trust his instincts. Tell him to watch the world around him more carefully. Tell him that he must not rely on just one plant or one crop. Tell him if he did that, he wouldn't be in as much trouble. Tell him to not always do what his neighbour is doing. Tell him to talk to other farmers. Tell him to listen to advice but make the best decisions for himself. Tell him about how the climate is changing. Tell him that climate change will compound the problems that already exist. Tell him that things may get worse. Tell him he must not allow himself to be more vulnerable. Tell him that he must adapt quickly.

I know he respects you. He danced in the fields when he heard of your victory. He danced with all of the other farmers. They sang songs of celebration that reverberated across this land. They chanted your name. Your messages of hope were theirs. Please come. Talk to him. He will listen to you. For I fear he has stopped listening to me.

Mr Obama, plants like me are the future. We will be the food that you eat, the home of your medicines, the fuels for your cars and if you let us flourish we will help you to clean up the air that we all live in. We are strong. We have been around much longer than you. We have seen these types of changes before, but never as fast as now. But we are also the solution to these problems. If you can listen to us, we have a lot to say. If you tell everyone to treat us the way we were treated in the past, you will see the difference. We are your hope. My keeper will listen to you. Speak in his language and give him back the skills to listen to language of the land.

# JOINT THIRD PLACE – ADULT

## Amy White
### *United States*

**Subject: CHILD LABOUR**

Dear President Obama,

I was little and we had recently moved to a new noisy city. It was dusty and sticky and crowded with laborers yelling in what my mother called "a local dialect"; I wouldn't be learning that new language, she had said I was too small. Winding through the streets, our air-conditioned car moved slowly past women with children attached to them and hanging on by their sides to their bright clothes. Men carried crates on their heads and sweat trickled down some people's temples. The walkers didn't seem to mind the close-by traffic, and no one moved away from us quickly. It was like the car wasn't even there, and everyone moved in slow motion. A boy with a goat on a rope tugged it past us, as we waited for a bicyclist with a small girl on the handlebars to cross.

We had been in the country for three days, and I would start school next week. I was excited to learn about multiplication and new animals; but I was not excited about the new uniform requirement.

"Sidney", my father had said that morning when I had found out about having to wear a blue and grey uniform, "a uniform is important here, that way they know you belong inside the gates at the school".

"But Daddy, why wouldn't I be inside, I'm a kid, our work is to go to school, isn't it?" He'd nodded, but sighed and asked me to be a good girl and get him his slippers.

Eventually, we turned off the pot-holed road and drove towards a residential part of the city, where it was quieter. Turning onto a side street with high gates, we stopped. We waited for the gates to be opened by a wiry man with a beret. He wasn't the real guard so he didn't have a gun; he was there to open the tall iron doors for us, in and out, in and out, all the days. Mother, Daddy and I had come to meet the Ambassador and her family. Her daughters and son already went to my new school. We drove onto the compound and saw grassy squares of lawn with unexpected bits of shade.

"Look Daddy!" I'd yelled with glee and amazement, "there's a boy in the tree! Is that the Ambassador's son?"

"I don't think so sweetie, I think he is a local boy, maybe he is the cook's son, or the guard's."

"Will he go to my school too?"

"No, Sidney, he won't."

"Where is his school then? Is it in the city in one of those flat shiny-tin-topped houses?"

"Maybe, I don't know. He may not have a school, he may work."

"Why can't he go to my school then? I like to climb trees too, maybe he can show me how to climb these knobby ones here."

He hadn't answered, and he and mother were climbing out of the car; I scrambled to keep up.

The first day of school had come. I had on my blue and grey dress and white collard shirt. In our dark car again, our guard closed the gates after us, and mother and I were driven out. Traffic was slow; I wondered if it would always be like this. Fumes from ancient trucks and beat-up old cars with people hanging out the windows filled my view. A cow was grazing by a traffic sign. Suddenly a kid tapped my window with a paper in his hand. He couldn't see me through the window, so he tapped again. An old man in a wheelchair with a crazy beard started yelling at our driver and holding up his hands. A woman moved the child aside and pushed some green fruit to the window talking quickly.

"What are they saying Mother?"

"They want to sell us things, they know we can afford what they have."

"Why us? They need to get to work and school, that boy will be late if he has to get rid of all of those newspapers first."

"They are at work. They know what our car means, that we are foreigners Sidney. Foreigners are the ones with money to them."

"I only have my piggy bank money, but it's at home. Will they come back to ask us again after school?" I'd asked eagerly.

"They will ask every day," she'd told me quietly.

Traffic picked up again, and we rolled past the wheel-chair man. A group of older girls in bright red uniforms walked by all looking like the other's twin. Dark hair pulled up, red skirts, and no socks with rubbery black shoes. Boys in beige followed next, taunting the girls loudly. The girls answered with shouts of giggles and pushed their chins into the air as they waved the boys away.

"Where is their school Mother?"

"I don't know; but they have a school, which is good."

She had answered me, but it had seemed more like she was talking to herself.

"Hey! They don't have uniforms!" I pointed towards a cluster of kids. A group of messy looking children, some in stained shirts and too-big flip-flops looked vacantly around the street, bobbing their heads, searching for something.

"There's the newspaper boy again! He's going towards them. Look!"

"He probably knows them, they may work together. Many children here, Sidney, go to work every day. In the whole world there are over 200 million children who have to go to work instead of school. It is even hard for Daddy and me to imagine that many kids, but it is true. Some work in factories, or markets, or fields, and others do sewing or cleaning; sometimes they work with their parents. See them following that group of boys in blue?" She pointed to an alley the students were moving down.

"The newspaper children know these boys don't have to go to work. Do you think they are proud to wear their uniforms?" she'd asked me.

"Yes, so everyone knows they have a school," I'd replied softly but fast.

Before she could say anything else, I'd blurted, "But how do they have jobs? They need school first! They can't work yet; they are too little!"

"I know baby, you're right to have so many questions. This is one thing Daddy and I will work on here. We get to come here and learn about this country and see how we can help them and their children. Our governments work together to help each other. Many of the parents of the kids you will be at school with here, do this kind of work too. Most people believe kids belong in schools, but that is not easy for everyone to do. The government here wants to help kids go to school but sometimes it is too hard for families to have food and their house unless everyone works."

"But why do I get to go to school?"

"Because you are a lucky girl. Kids get to go to school in our country and in other countries that are rich places, but some kids still have to work very hard. Here, and in lots of countries that are poor, school isn't a part of life for them, it is a luxury."

"I like my uniform," I'd said while smoothing my dress.

I'd looked up at my mother saying, "Maybe we can help some of the newspaper kids to go to school, do you think?"

"I hope so, Sid."

We had arrived at the gates, and the car was slowing.

"Here we are." She'd been smiling, but had seemed a bit sad too. "Thank you Mr. Billy." She'd said to our driver as we got out.

The front of the school was brick, and had seemed more like a big house than a school to me. All the cars were similar to ours, and several different languages shouted good-byes to drivers, parents and nannies, as doors slammed shut. The guards at these gates were like all the other guards I'd seen, wiry and wearing berets. No one else on the street wore a beret it seemed. There were uniforms of all kinds everywhere. The wall around the school was brick like the building, but the side of the iron-gate at the front of the entrance was just wide enough for an arm to fit through. A guard swatted at a little upturned hand that had slid through the bars after the gates had closed shut from our car's arrival. He was younger than me and wore green shorts and a tank top. I could see him walking away from the guard's dismissal, but then he turned around and waved. I waved back, and jumped up a little to be sure he saw me. He paused, and then ran away, kicking up dust as he flew down the street; and I took my mother's hand and we went up the stairs and inside.

# SHORTLIST – ADULT

## Togba Rodney Davies
*Liberia*

**Subject:** CHILD LABOUR

Dear Mr. President:

Kindly permit me to convey to your Excellency a message from someone who succeeded in contacting you only by luck of the Irish. Before I do, however, I would like to introduce circumstances leading to this request being made.

I live in Buchanan, a coastal city in Southern Liberia, West Africa. On a cold morning in late February, I awoke before sunrise and set out for a seaside shanty town where fish from the Atlantic Ocean is unloaded before being taken to the local market. I went to Fanti Town to intercept the fishermen before they got to the market where the vertebrate is sold more expensively.

Hardly had I reached the seashore when I caught sight of a lad standing a couple of meters from the margins of the waves. He must be the son of one of the many women scattered about, I thought. I was mistaken. The lad was unaccompanied and on his daily routine. And as the next canoe approached moments later, the boy rushed out into the sea water to help drag the craft ashore. This task secured him a handful of tiny "bonies" which he carefully placed in an empty rice bag fastened to his waist. I then realized: he was instead a little "boa-ay", one of those well built darkskin children who beach canoes in exchange for bits of left over fish.

Courage at such a tender age was what stole away my attention from my early morning assignment. I watched in amazement as the child diligently applied himself to this seemingly life-saving activity. For the few hours that followed, the lad shuttled between the shadow sea water and the sandy beach, leaving no stone unturned, till he had accumulated an adequate amount of fish to cover the day's expenses. He then untied the rice bag which served as a storage facility for his successive remunerations and headed to the shade of a coconut tree. There, he wore a pair of oversized lady slippers, each foot different in color and design from the other. He was departing the seashore.

As he walked away, I abandoned my fish-fetching expedition and set out to discover this intriguing character. "Baby Boa-ay" was born some time around 1997. His parents lost sight of him amidst the exodus as they fled fighting in the interior of the Country when he was about six years old. He was later identified by a neighbor who brought him to Buchanan in the hope of reuniting him with his family. Till date, that has not happened. And more painfully, a few years later, Baby Boa-ay' s guardian informed him that from then on, all she could afford him was a place to sleep, as she herself found it difficult to meet her needs as well as those of her two little daughters. In other words, Baby Boa-ay would be responsible to feed himself, clothe himself, and whenever the need arose, provide himself medication.

By the way, "Baby Boa-ay" is not his real name. He earned this nickname not only as a consequence of his activity at the beach, but especially because people are either not familiar with or not interested in his real name - Junior. To ensure a living, Junior wakes up as early as 5:00 a.m. every morning and goes down to the beach, not wanting to miss the arrival of the earliest fleet. He stays at the beach until his desired quantity of fish is acquired, which is after daybreak. Once this quota achieved, Junior proceeds to poor communities where he sells his "catch" at usually low prices in order to provide his daily bread.

As we walked along, I inquired of the kid whether he was pleased with his living condition, a question to which he replied in the negative. With that, I seized the opportunity and introduced you to this lad, Mr. President, as "the biggest man in the biggest country" in the whole world. Then I asked him what assistance he would appreciate receiving from you. I'm not sure what image was drawn up in his mind. But with tears in his eyes and sweat streaming down his innocent face, the lad sighed, smiled and eventually murmured. His words were barely understood: "Tell him I want to go to school."

Junior is not the only child enduring such plight. Thousands of Liberian children face the harsh conditions of life without protection on a daily basis. Like Junior, they aim to provide themselves a more descent living condition. To achieve this, some transport goods and wares in wheelbarrows, while others who are "less fortunate" to get hold of the cart, use their heads, backs or shoulders for the same purpose.

These children suffer other harsh forms of labor including farming, latex tapping, mud digging, brick molding, and rock crushing. Prostitution is the main tempter of young girls. Some, as young as 14, for whom the above-mentioned physical jobs seem too hard to do see this activity as the way out of their misery. They give their bodies in exchange for money, if not for disease or death, as they are often exposed to sexually transmitted diseases and sometimes lured into being murdered for ritualistic purpose.

Street selling remains the activity which impedes the physical as well as mental development of the kids. Not only do they strain under the weight of the usually heavy containers of merchandise they carry, a good number of them sell the whole day, suggesting a certain level of unwillingness on the part of their "employers" to work out a parallel academic schedule which would enable them to eventually bid farewell to their present state.

Though not the only factor responsible, poverty is the major contributor to the horrendous living condition these children experience. When interviewed, most of the kids affirm that they are self-supported, as their parents are either dead or missing, as a result of war – as in the case of Junior – HIV AIDS, accident or some other natural disaster; and even worse, that some have "a family" to sustain. Like little Junior, these children are not satisfied living in such a condition, but are condemned by fate to do so. They are victims of destiny.

Nevertheless, I believe all is not yet lost. Regardless of how disastrous their situation may be, someone can do something to rescue these potential doctors, lawyers, or even presidents from devastation. And this must begin at the highest level. That is why I mentioned you to that poverty-stricken child in the first place, Mr. President.

Junior, like countless other Liberian children, is in desperate need of your assistance. Your intervention in the lives of these children is paramount, if they are to enjoy a more meaningful future. Mr. President, these children must be rescued! These children who generally appear much older than their Western counterparts, due not only to the intense scorching of the African sun, but also to the physical and emotional load they carry on a daily basis. These children on whose faces one reads a million expressions: of pain, of sorrow, but also of hope. These children… Yes, these children!

Can you in any way, Mr. President, assist these children realize the true meaning of being a child?

Kind regards,

Togba Rodney Davies
Buchanan, Liberia

# SHORTLIST – ADULT

# Tony Devlin
*Ireland*

### Subject: WORLD HUNGER

Dear President Obama,

I thought I'd write to you in the form of a story, and old one, about how there's always enough, if we but feel the power of change in our hearts. I hope you like the story, it's called:

### Bread

It was evening. The sun's disk had slipped behind the shoulders of the hills and the pale sky, now empty, was losing its lustre. The beginnings of a night breeze lifted coolly from the waters below them.

The Teacher no longer spoke but stood, still, on the hillside where for hour upon hour he had mesmerised the great throng with his stories, inspiring them with a dazzling vision of a heaven come to earth.

His calm silence still held all eyes as he gazed out over the rippling waters, into the distance, toward the dim outline of the farther shore. He seemed no longer aware of them, and gradually the edges of the wide semi-circle of listeners around him began to fray.

They had streamed after him in their hundreds as he strode through the towns and villages in the bright noon-time. They had accompanied him in a spirit of happy carnival along the sweeping shore and out to this distant place. Captivated by his words, elated by his energy and his passion, they had clustered around him, oblivious of the passage of time, unconscious of their surroundings.

But all was changing now. The light of wonder, the bright shining images of his new world of blessings and plenty were fading, and in the chill air of the declining day they were all once more the captive creatures of their own mundane humanity. They were hungry now, tired too, and thirsty. And it was this discomfort which nagged first at the edges of the crowd and then began to spread, in restless movement inwards to where the Twelve were sitting, ranged around their master.

"They have nothing to eat." It was the brothers James and John who rose to stand before the Teacher, their words a question and a challenge. "Tell us what to do, for many now are far from their homes."

The Teacher seemed not to hear them at first. Nor did he seem to hear the murmuring among the thousands now spread across the sloping ground, nor to see the beginnings of the great crowd's dispersal.

The sound of a child crying, the discontented wail of a hungry infant could be heard, and soon was joined by others until a sound like the bleating of many lambs rose from every side.

And then, just as it seemed that the disintegration of the great gathering was inevitable, the Teacher spread his arms wide and spoke in that voice of power, a voice that hushed the rising babble in an instant. "Stay", he called out, "let all be seated. We shall eat together. Stay."

There was a further wave of murmuring and the rustle of clothing and the many small sounds of movement becoming still, as all were seated, watching, and waiting.

The Teacher looked from face to face among the Twelve and saw their unease. "We have little," muttered Thomas, "and none to share …"

It seemed as if the whole multitude had become collectively aware of its hunger. Where previously all had stood, intermingled, a great fan of faces spread around the Teacher, receiving his words, captivated, sharing the great up-welling of wonderment, the glimpses of paradise he had conjured before them, now the crowd was fragmenting.

Family groups were reforming, neighbours clustered together, small circles facing inwards, giving their backs to the rest. Here and there water skins and small parcels of food began to appear. But there were many who sat apart, empty handed, solitary and bereft.

"Bring what we have," the Teacher said quietly and when, in a single basket, he received the five loaves and two dried fishes which were all they could muster between them, he held it high for all to see and spoke to them:

"Blessed is the food You give us to eat, Lord of the heavens and the earth. Blessed are we gathered here to receive it. Let us be to others as You have been to us, and let us share in brotherhood the good things of the earth."

He held the basket aloft for a few moments more and then called out: "Send the children to me."

From all sides the patter of small feet and the piping of young voices converged on him. Taking the basket he began to move among the young expectant faces, and for each he had a smile, a blessing and a morsel of food. Peter, beside him, fretted as the loaves and fish were broken apart and distributed. Soon there would be nothing remaining and still the children streamed in from the edges of the crowd. The Twelve looked helplessly, one to the other. How would all this end?

The Teacher moved in the circle of the children's expectant faces. His basket held little more than crumbs and crusts and small fragments of fish. He paused and lifted his gaze to the crowd beyond. "Who will help me feed these children?" he called.

"Who stands with me and who will open his hand to the need of his brother?"

All were silent. Here and there, well-fleshed merchants, fishermen, tradesmen from the towns, glanced warily around them. They held their satchels close, their families clustered round them. A woman whispered urgently to her husband, her fingers pressing on his arm. "We have none to spare," he hissed back, his words bleak, his tone complaining in the chill of the declining light.

Then, nearby, a young woman was on her feet, snatching a cloth bundle from the grasp of her own father, calling to her sister for the water skin which she held, and she advanced to the Teacher, the bundle in one hand, the skin in the other, holding them out, her face determined yet radiant with a glow that answered his.

"Behold," he called out, "I was hungry, and you gave me to eat, thirsty and you gave me to drink. The Lord has blessed this day."

Dates, bread, some figs came tumbling from the young woman's bundle as she tipped it into the Teacher's basket and then stood beside him as he began again to feed the children, offering her water to all who were thirsty.

After some moments a burly fisherman of middle years pushed his way to where the Teacher stood and added a parcel of dried fish, more bread and a half filled wine skin. The Teacher grasped him by the arm as he turned away and looked deep into his eyes for a moment. Then the two exchanged broad smiles and the man turned to call out: "Bring what you have, and all shall have their fill!"

More people began to come forward and the Twelve were filling more baskets and moving out into the crowd to distribute the food and drink that now came literally pouring in.

The distribution, the smiles and the infectious gaiety went rippling out from where the Teacher stood, surrounded still by the children, until the whole hillside was astir with laughter and open-handed sharing as the familial and social separations of all present dissolved into a brief and blissful time of divine folly, a generosity that suddenly gave no thought for the morrow, but gloried in the warmth and fellow-feeling of souls now wondrously at one. "Truly, heaven has come to earth," observed an old woman, leaning on the arm of the youth beside her, eyes bright and childlike with the wonder of it all.

The sun was long gone and the moon rode high in the vaulted sky as finally the Twelve gathered around the Teacher again, their baskets full to overflowing with the leftovers of the great communal meal.

Smiling and relaxed, the Teacher raised his arms and his voice: "Go in peace," he called, "love one another, as the Father has loved you." And he stood watching, as the great throng dispersed, moving like gleaming shoals under the moon's silvering light. Here and there a torch was held aloft and the happy sound of many voices and the tinkling laughter of women and young children drifted back to the near-empty hillside.

"Let us sleep here, beneath the sky of this blessed night," said the Teacher, "for we have seen the action of God's grace, we have seen a world transformed, in the breaking and sharing of bread. Truly now the time is nigh, the acceptable year of the Lord approaches, and the days of grace are coming to pass."

And all through the countryside, through the towns and all the way to the great city, the story spread, of the miracle, of the loaves and the fishes, the feeding of five thousand. And the name of the miracle they gifted to the Teacher, forgetful, and fearful too, of the goodness they had found and felt grow in themselves.

# SHORTLIST – ADULT

# Mukhopadhyay Sugata
*India*

### Subject: World Hunger

Dear Mr. President,

Let me tell you a story. This is a story of a woman who got HIV from her husband. There are so many stories of poor women who were infected by the husband. What is so special about it?

From that aspect my story will sound a pretty ordinary one. But to me it is not only shocking but can give us a hard lesson of life. Let's go into the story.

"Sandhya [name changed] was in her early thirties, living with her husband and two children in one of the medium sized cities in South India. Her husband was working in private sector and having a good income. They had a happy life.

But things were not the same. Sandhya's husband suddenly fell ill and the ailment in course of time got turned into a chronic one. The man who had a robust health previously underwent very rapid loss of weight, swollen glands in the body and not easily curable fever and loose motion. The physician finally got the HIV test done which came to be reactive.

Unfortunately he died irrespective of attempts from the doctors and Sandhya with her two kids were forced to shift to her in-laws house.

In the meantime Sandhya also had gone through HIV testing and found to be positive. And then things got worse. Her in-laws threw her and her two small kids out of the house. They thought Sandhya is woman of immoral character and actually passed the virus to her husband to cause his premature death.

Sandhya was literally came into the roads. She did neither find support from her parents, relatives nor find a job. Nobody likes to put a HIV infected into the job.

When hunger became intolerable with the two small innocent children to feed with Sandhya had taken the boldest decision of her life. She became a prostitute."

So the crux of the story is, if you are hungry, your off springs are hungry but at the same time denied all sources of food what best you can do to survive? Forget the so called "morality" of life and jump into anything that can generate source of living for the survival.

I told the story to one of my good friends who is a strong feminist. Her reaction was, "I would have definitely committed suicide with my children before getting myself into such dehumanizing act." I was simply surprised the way she responded.

But in reality how many hungry people kill themselves when humiliation goes beyond tolerance? Rather, most of them put all their attempts together to survive against all odds. After all, living is loving.

Sandhya did not do anything different. She tried to provide food to her children's hungry mouth and dreamt of better future for them. Please don't look at Sandhya's story through the lens of morality.

My issue is not related to morality or sex work. It is insecurity of food that makes people vulnerable to HIV. Sandhya is one of such vulnerable women but throughout the globe there are millions of people who do not have enough food for them or their children. AIDS is constantly knocking at their doors.

Experts say there is enough food in the world to feed everyone. But where has all this food gone?

More than 800 million people on earth know what it is like to go to bed hungry. Around 200 million children under 5 years are underweight only because there is not enough food for them. One child dies every five seconds from hunger and related cause. Thirty-five per cent of the total population is malnourished in several countries located in East, Central and Southern Africa. In India, which produces enough food for its people, there are still incidences of death from hunger, selling of children out of sheer poverty and food insecurity.

If you analyze carefully the food insecurity business you will find a demoralizing picture existing in all corners of the globe.

Food insecurity, most of the time, is man made and inevitably leads to disruption of human integrity thus generating numerous marginalized, hard-to-reach population all over the world, left with hunger and humiliation. Never-ending war of DR Congo, political violence of Haiti, socio-political instability in Somalia, Sudan, Uganda, civil conflict and illegal drug trade of Colombia, war that devastated health system of Ivory coast, restless Chechnya, war that tore apart Iraq and Afghanistan, power game and proxy war by the "World Powers" – the list is long but the number of people denied access to food through these unending pathological processes is countless. The human community is further fragmented by social and domestic violence, terrorism, communalism, racism, casteism, gender inequity and troubled childhood thus enhancing pace of hunger. Hunger is the natural triggering mechanism of dehumanizing events like human trafficking, prostitution, crime, drugs, child labor and migration pushing millions of hopeless people into vacuum of AIDS. On the other hand, those already infected by HIV are constantly refrained from producing and utilizing food, being victimized by disability, denial and discrimination. And the cycle goes on incessantly to make the virus stronger and deadlier.

This Hunger-HIV cycle is gradually taking shape of ultimate destroyer and silently preparing ground to make final assault in the form of AIDS. No other disease has taken so much of resources, attention and concern because AIDS has jolted the root of humanity and exposed the darker side of human civilization. Hungry, vulnerable people also remain miles away from critical information vital for living. HIV can be easily renamed as "Hunger and Ignorance led Vulnerability".

Sandhya's story is a perfect example of Hunger-HIV cycle.

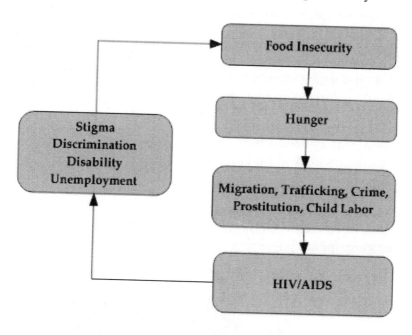

Breaking Hunger-HIV cycle is probably the toughest challenge in front of us. I strongly believe that it is neither condoms, ARV drugs, microbicides nor vaccines but uninterrupted supply of food with sufficient quantity to the needy and hungry people of the world that can really make the true difference in reversing the pandemic of AIDS and many other communicable diseases.

Are our powerful global leaders sufficiently prepared and equipped to bring necessary changes in the food production, distribution and utilization processes and patterns? It needs concrete political commitment at international, national, state, district and sub district levels.

When billions of dollars are being spent for space research, weapon technology, nuclear plants and sophisticated biological inventions countless hopeless people are dying simply because of lack of accessibility, availability and affordability to food – the basic vital source of human existence. Do our respected leaders feel the contrast?

The world has basically two groups of people: One who earns more and the other who earns less or does not earn. The first groups sometimes make money in trillions and billions. The second group many times can not even earn in terms of a two digit number. Can the leaders of the world make a balance between the two absolutely polarized money earning patterns?

I am not politician. I am not a public leader. I am just a physician who is practicing public health and epidemiology. Whatever I have documented so far is my deliberation from the perspective of public health and, over and above, from the point of humanity.

Dr Sugata Mukhopadhyay
New Delhi, India

# PASSAGES, EXTRACTS, QUOTES
# – ADULT CATEGORY

## Anna McElwee
*Ireland*

### Subject: WORLD HUNGER

Your predecessor, President John F. Kennedy, speaking in 1963 said: "We have the ability, as members of the human race, we have the means, we have the capacity to eliminate hunger from the face of the earth in our lifetime. We need only the will." The former world leader knew that hunger is not a result of food scarcity on our planet, and that hunger is instead caused by failure to use our competent ability to work towards a solution. Hunger has not been eliminated in the forty-five years since President Kennedy spoke these words, but now is not the time to look back on the failures of the past. Now is the time to look to the future with hope and with expectation for success. The future will only hold abundance of food for all if we do something now. Now is the time for the solution. Now is the time for the will. But most importantly, more than ever before, now is the time for the action.

I am writing to you as a human being, a world citizen no different from the people who are fighting starvation today. Unlike these people, I do not know what it is like to be hungry, but I still share compassion and a hunger for righteousness for those who are. One million people died as a result of a famine, also known as the Great Hunger, in my native country over 150 years ago. Although Ireland was a very different place a century and a half ago, it is painful to know that so many Irish people died simply because they did not have enough to eat. The Ireland that I know is very different, food is plentiful, and the vast majority of its inhabitants remain distant from the possibility of facing a hunger so severe it could prove fatal. But thousands of miles away in Sub Saharan Africa and Southern Asia, human beings are suffering from the same disease that killed their ancestors. Time and distance may separate the hungry from the fed, but we are all one. We share one thing, a heritage, a country, or a world. We must begin to share our compassion. In order to save lives, we must take serious action and share our resources. Now is the time to do that.

President Kennedy spoke with conviction in 1963 when he told the world that freedom from starvation is possible, and Truman knew the importance of this freedom. The USA has led the way before in preventing the deaths of millions facing chronic hunger, and it must do so again, by taking well coordinated action. The developing regions of the world have been faced with hunger for long enough. Now it is time for the developed world to hunger for the rights of others. We must set free one billion people in this world from the chains of hunger. We must crave the elimination of hunger related diseases and deaths, regardless of what era or country we live in. We must hunger for abundance of food for all in this world, knowing that the solutions are clear and that they lie in the present. All that is required is urgent action and political will, President Obama. You must act now to prevent 16,000 malnourished children facing death tomorrow.

# Tom Smith
*Ireland*

## Subject: WORLD HUNGER

Let's bring this down to a personal level, to emphasise the reality. Your father is from Nyanza Province in Kenya. Nyanza has a population size roughly comparable to my own country, Ireland. Yet of that population, well over 50 per cent of people are living below that miserable poverty line of a dollar a day. Do you know what the per capita annual GDP of my country was for 2008? It was over $42,000, 115 times as much as the previously mentioned $1 per day line of poverty. On top of this, the province is without doubt the most severely hit by the HIV/AIDS epidemic in Kenya.

Why should you care? Well, if you do your research you'll find that a third of children orphaned by the disease in the region, and left vulnerable to it, are malnourished to the point of having stunted growth, showing signs of wasting, and being under-weight. This lack of sufficient nutritious food will have even more serious implications for these children if and when they too succumb to the disease (the probability is high). It disturbed me greatly to recently hear a woman describe taking antiretroviral (ARV) drugs on an empty stomach as being "like digesting razor blades", which is what a large proportion of these children will be effectively condemned to. Without getting into polemics, simply put, it could be you. Multiply this impact not by thousands, but by millions and that is the injustice we're looking at.

As Amartya Sen, the Indian economist, is this year celebrating ten years of being a Nobel Laureate I think it is vitally important to revisit his wise words: "Starvation is the characteristic of some people not having enough food to eat. It is not the characteristic of there being not enough food to eat." Put simply, there is plenty of food on this little planet to feed all who live on it; getting access to that food is the problem. Food production has basically outstripped population growth globally for longer than you or I have been alive. Unfortunately, it's the tragedy of our age that I can instantaneously have my asparagus flown in from Peru and my cherry tomatoes flown to me from Spain, but we can't manage to get basic sufficient food to a starving child in *insert almost any country in the Majority world here*.

So, what would I specifically ask you to do, Mr. Obama? Despite what you might think, solutions are not that hard to come by, given the political will. Open your country completely to tariff-free imports from the least developed countries (LDCs). Allow and aid such countries, through a backtracking of WTO rules, to support their agricultural producers with export subsidies and other supports. Stop the hypocrisy and make your own country's agricultural subsidies a thing of the past to stop undermining farmers in the Global South. In partnership with other governments, address the lack of transparency among transnational companies (TNCs) that allows them, through tax evasion and other means, to steal $160 billion of potentially life-saving revenue annually from "developing" countries (this figure is far more than global Official Development Assistance). Work to ensure that countries in the Global South get what they are owed from Western TNCs for the extraction of natural resources. For example, in 2006 the Democratic Republic of Congo, an exceedingly resource-rich country, received a mere $86,000 from mineral rights – $86,000! Yet 80 per cent of the DRC's population are below the poverty line and millions of people are starving. In short, make fair trade the norm and not the exception.

# Jenny McCarthy
*Ireland*

## Subject: CHILD LABOUR

James and Danielle smiled lovingly at one another as the elderly jeweller took the shining gold ring from beneath the glass counter top. The diamond twinkled in the light as Danielle slipped it on to her finger. "A perfect fit!" the smiling jeweller exclaimed.

"I should hope so, at that price!" James thought to himself, trying not to look at the €25,000 price tag. His face didn't betray these thoughts to Danielle however, who looked as though all her Christmases had come at once.

"Honey, I love it!" she squealed, holding out her hand to admire her prize.

"It looks beautiful miss, really something" the jeweller nodded.

James took Danielle's hand and kissed it. "We'll take it".

Bolivia, South America.

As another shower of dust and stones showered him, Manuel felt his throat closing up. He leaned against the wall of the mine, desperately trying to calm himself down and open his lungs. Sometimes, if he turned his face back towards the cave entrance, there was a little air there, but sometimes not.

He had come to the mine at dawn with his mother and sisters. His sisters, aged 6 and 8, worked in the river nearby sifting through silt and gravel for particles or pieces of gold. Manuel's mother also worked in the river with her two young daughters. Manuel's father had died two years before, when one of the mines collapsed after heavy rainfall, killing twenty workers. Manuel couldn't remember how long he had been working there; it seemed like an eternity. He was so absorbed by it now, so overcome with exhaustion that he never thought to question why he had to work there. Why his mother and sisters had to work there. Why his father had to die.

# Brendan O'Dwyer
*Ireland*

### Subject: WORLD HUNGER

January 21st, 2033

Today is the 25th anniversary of your historic inauguration as the 44th President of the United States, and it is this anniversary that motivates me to write this letter. "The world is changing," you declared on that fateful day. How much change, Mr Obama, you never specified.

I didn't vote for you back in 2008. I didn't vote for the other guy either. You see I was just a 7-year-old girl back then and was more interested in your youngest daughter. I remember seeing her on the TV and thinking that we could be friends. You seemed like a nice man and a kind father to her. I also remember the change you were promising and how it made me feel. You see, Mr Obama, I desperately needed some change in my life and even though I didn't know how you could affect my circumstances, you gave me hope and inspired hope in those around me.

When my mother went into hospital on September 10th 2001 to give birth, everything was perfect.

I was born minutes after the second plane struck the World Trade Centre only a few blocks away. As my mother was pushing me into this world, my father was receiving the news that the world had changed. The world they planned for us to live in no longer existed.

I can only imagine how my mother held me to her breast as the wards around her filled up with broken bodies and shattered lives. The first breaths or air I took were shared with the dying and were contaminated with the smell of scorched flesh. It was amid this chaos, I'm told, that my mother named me Hope.

… So, what I'm really getting at, the real reason I'm writing this letter, is that I need to know how you feel. Or more to the point, I need to know THAT you feel! If you could've seen the future, a world of starvation and disease and depravation, would you have done things differently? Could you have really changed the script?

# Tom O'Gorman
*Ireland*

## Subject: GLOBAL WARMING

We in Ireland are looking to you for leadership on so many issues and problems that bedevil our world today. My country is experiencing what might politely be termed a void in leadership at this moment in time .We are looking to you as a surrogate leader as we stumble through the wreckage of an economy that has been wrecked by profligate lending and over ambitious development. Reading a newspaper leaves us depressed and resigned to years of recession, never mind ever increasing global warming, fanned by empty hot air promises by politicians on reaching Kyoto deadlines. War is destroying the Middle East and our reaction is either to ignore it or make it worse.

Obama, we need a leader like never before. Can you take up the reins where Roosevelt and Kennedy left off? We need you to reduce your emissions by as much as you are asked … now! You can convince the American people to reject the "bury the head in the sand" theory on global warming.

# Sonia Bonelli
*Ireland*

### Subject: CHILD LABOUR

Can I take a few minutes of your time to think about what a loss you would be to the world were you born somewhere and sometime else? Say, somewhere less fortunate like the Congo or Darfur, where you could join one of the growing number of child soldiers that are currently in existence right now in this time – 300,000 in the last decade alone accounted for. Never mind the unknown soldiers. Like the child Mani.

Like some child soldiers, he was recruited (kidnapped) when he was nine. Prior to this, his life was as normal as you can expect when you are born into poverty in a third world country. But, he was happy in the village of his birth with his family, his mother, father and four siblings, two brothers and two sisters. He had even begun to learn at school, which he should have been as he was the most intelligent in his age group. Even though there were whisperings of trouble and stories of fighting they were relatively peaceful times until the day the soldiers came.

He was just finished playing with the group of boys from the village when it happened. The ball got punctured and now they were looking to play the hunting game. The big truck arrived under a cloud of dust and noise, filled with the soldiers and the guns. Utter fear made him stay instead of running. They had shot one of the boys for doing just that in front of them. So he lined up with the others as their friend lay dying 60 metres from them.

... How many great people are lost every day because of forced child labour, people who could have all the solutions to the world's problems, dying before their time and not receiving their chance to fulfil their potential. Cures for diseases, negotiators, teachers and thinkers, all lost for nothing, locked away in brilliant minds. People like Mani and the other 300,000 children in the last decade who live and die to work for someone else. Even the lucky ones who get to live but did not get the education and guidance in time. The mental aside from physical scars will haunt them and their families for the remainder of their lives.

The economic benefit alone of eradicating child labour would outweigh the cost of child labour six times to one in a twenty year period. If we don't do more there may be a generation of children who will completely lose their humanity and that does not bode well for all our children's future.

So, I'll put it to you again, President Obama, imagine if you were Mani and the world lost the great hope and noble prospects that you have come to represent to your people and the people of the world in this ever increasing time of uncertainty.

# Ali Hassan Jim'ale

*Somalia*

## Subject: WORLD HUNGER

... and America gave the whole world (both its friends and enemies) a vivid lesson by electing Barack Hussein Obama as the President of the United States of America, the most powerful and the leading country in the battle against the empire of poverty and hunger!

Not only millions but billions of peoples, having a variety of priorities around the world, were following the incredible event! Some wanted justice, some wanted freedom, some wanted peace, some wanted education, some wanted good health, some wanted a green globe, but most important some wanted food to save their lives from the Hell of Hunger. On that day His Royal Highness, The King of the Kingdom of Poverty and Hunger, and Head of one of the leading Organizations in the fight against the Worldwide Hunger and Poverty, together were watching the event in his Palace, the biggest and the most beautiful Palace ever built in the history of the Kingdom of Poverty and Hunger, made up of thousands of tents and shacks of hunger, poverty, starvation, hunger killed human skeletons, and hungry human beings! But each had his own unique concern towards Mr. Obama: one saw him as a real Threat to the existence and extent of his Palace and Kingdom to the point that he got shocked and sick, and the other saw him as a new Hope and Chance to demolish that Palace and the whole Kingdom of Poverty and Hunger!

Since then, His Royal Highness lies on his bed, suffering continuous convulsions, hallucinations, disappointments, anger and complete speechless except two sentences: "I am afraid that he will end our Kingdom!", "I am afraid that he will move America and the whole World against our Empire!"

So, Mr President, will you really end the evil Kingdom of Poverty and Hunger? Will you make it convulse? Or at least will you stop its expansion? Will you move America and the International community to take dramatic and effective steps to protect that mother and father in Asia, Latin America, Africa and in some parts of Europe who are forced to give their beloved baby in exchange of hundreds of dollars to save the rest of their destitute family from dying of hunger and starvation?

That is really what both the hunger and poverty stricken parties of the world and those who have concern and commitment to their support and salvation are waiting from you, Mr President. Of course, there is no magic and overnight solution for the chronic hell of hunger and poverty. Nevertheless, many believe that you can take real tangible actions against world poverty and hunger by using your authority.

# Marilyn Alcorn
*United States*

### Subject: WORLD HUNGER

Mr. President Sir, I am a product of a tradesman education. I am a retired journeyman painter. And as a member of a traditionally "under-represented" population, I am also a pioneer. I am among the first and the few women to retire as a Golden Gate Bridge Painter. Following retirement I went back to school to become a teacher of mathematics at the Secondary Level. I am nearing within two years of earning another retirement. I hope to go from there to take on full time ministry and writing. So, as you can see,

I believe in being productive. As a single-parent, I have been raising my three children alone for the past 14 years and I am now a single grandparent who is helping to encourage my children to be supportive and income producers of their newly developing families.

As a leader, teacher, and as a parent, I do not want to give my children a reason to think that it is ok to be forever a consumer and never a producer. I just pray that you will likewise consider the above. Our nation is a great nation and I feel that you would agree with me in wanting to keep it that way for our future generations. All of humanity should be encouraged and trained to enjoy the fruits of their labor and not that of others. We as a nation, as I said before, do not live alone in this world, we are all part of a global community. Theoretically, it has been said that a chain is only as strong as its weakest link. How strong do we as a nation want to be?

# Esther Pew
## United States

### Subject: WORLD HUNGER

Sitting in this restaurant, it would be hard to imagine that there are people around the world dying from lack of food. Watching the obese man gnaw on that turkey leg like a dog chewing on a bone makes my stomach curl. Watching the waiter take the half-empty plate to the kitchen, most likely to throw the food out, makes me want to stand up and shout about it. Watching people that take home leftovers that will most likely only sit in the refrigerator and will only be disposed of when it starts to smell makes me feel sick. How can these people eat and waste so much? Are they oblivious to what happens around the world? They don't even have to go to another country to see the signs of starvation.

Walk outside of the restaurant. Take a right, a left – it doesn't really matter. Walk a few blocks. Look around you. There are people here that are hungry, people here that could benefit from the amount of food that is wasted. You may not even have to walk a few blocks. There may be someone outside of the restaurant, hoping to find some food scraps to help quench the feeling of constant hunger pains. Picture someone's face shriveled, each individual rib visible to the naked eye through their skin from lack of food. People like this live in the United States, not just in Africa or any other country. Men, women and children alike are dying from starvation – something that I believe could easily be avoided.

It's so ironic that a lot of the population of the United States is suffering from obesity, eating too much, while there are a lot of people suffering from starvation, not eating enough. How can we help to change the world? Why is it that children have to go to sleep at night, not having anything to eat for a day, or more? Why don't people care more?

Most of the people who will read this essay will never know what it feels like to be starving. Sure, at least once in their life they have been guilty of stating something like, "When's dinner? I'm starving!" I remember my little brother making this exact statement, and my parents replying – "you're not really starving!" We're just hungry when statements like this are made; we don't really know what starving actually feels like.

# Niketa Kumar
*United States*

## Subject: CHILD LABOUR

There is a story from India about how the earth became forested, about how blankets of green slowly spread across the planet. In the tale, the godly beings, Mahadev and Gauri, both land on Earth and walk in opposite directions planting seeds at every step until they meet again. The process is painstakingly long, but as the pair move away from each other, they also know that they are ultimately moving closer together again. Step by step.

The development of India takes a page from this centuries old story, and it also highlights the country's biggest challenge. Economic growth is no longer categorized under the reign of the future. However, as the development process continues the gap between the poor and the rich grows exponentially faster. They are moving away from each other. And all the while, promises of coming together on a newly crafted world are discussed in political forums, newspapers and consumer analysis reports.

Still, the challenge remains and is hard to ignore. What to do with the majority of the population that is not part of India's aspiring middle class or glamorous elite? How can the fruits of globalization and development be spread across the country's 1.12 billion? What kind of system will work to provide the basic necessities for one segment of the population while at the same time support a billionaire's plan to build a sixty-story house a few streets away? One of the most tragic obstacles in addressing this economic separation is mitigating the harsh effects felt by India's youth population. Governmental agencies and NGOs estimate that more than 12 million children in India under the age of 14 are at least part time employed in child labor positions. India has the highest number of children occupied by paid labor than any other country.

The prevalence of child labor in India is undoubtedly linked to market trends, specialized economies and job availability. Many children are forced to leave school early and join the workforce to support their families who are increasingly compromised by rampant poverty and a scarcity of accessible high skilled and paying jobs.

The prevalence of child labor is a tragic symptom of rapidly developing economies with large populations and limited access to an adequate and consistent education. While increasingly globalized markets and a growth across a wide-range of tech-based industries is important for securing the world's economic future, we must not forget about the isolated populations which have yet to receive the fruits of these lauded developments. Through collaboration among institutions of education and vocational training, international and national NGOs, governmental agencies, international institutions , corporations and world business leaders, we have the power to establish a new foundation for public education in India and lift the tragic burden of child labor off so much of its youth.

Not unlike the mythical journey of Mahadev and Gauri, it is now time to begin walking back, closer to one another, and on a fresh ground of new opportunities and promise.

# Sheelagh Mooney
*Ireland*

## Subject: WORLD HUNGER

Doesn't it seem quite unbelievable that in a time when we in the so called developed world watch markets crash and worry over our pensions and investments, some 960 million people of the world still do not have access to enough food to avoid daily hunger or even starvation. While rates of obesity continue to rise in Western countries others in developing nations die of hunger and starvation. And why is this? Everyday we hear the media perpetuate the myth that it is because of food scarcity, natural disasters or massive uncontrolled population explosions. These myths are not just untrue but downright dangerous as they make us feel helpless in the face of such insurmountable problems. But the truth is the world is awash with food and every day mountains of food is driven to dumps to rot. And many natural disasters turn out to be quite an opportunity for the rich and almost always the disaster is limited to the poorest only. And as for population explosions, most uncontrolled population growth is a consequence of social inequities rather than the cause of poverty and hunger.

Could it be that hunger has more to do with the unequal access to democracy, could it be that we have shaped education in these countries to make people think that Western ways are the only ways? Do we benefit from the hunger of the poorest of the poor knowing that they will work for less and sell their commodities such as coffee, cocoa or bananas for very little. Are we more worried about the effects on our pensions rather than world hunger when we hear of governments in developing countries who set about nationalising vast tracks of land owned by foreign companies? Do we in short have a overt or covert vested interest in keeping the poor poor?

I remember a sentence that I read many years ago that to truly understand the problems of the poor one should *study the rich and powerful not the poor and powerless*, i.e. concentrate on those who hold the power. What we in the developed countries sometimes forget is that to the real poor we the ordinary citizens of developed nations are part of that elite and powerful. Understanding the issues and debunking the myths is a good place to start.

And so I am asking you President Obama, as one who has roots in both the developed and developing world, to use your considerable influence to highlight the real issues. It is easy to put money into an overseas aid budget but more difficult to make real change where it counts, to take ones courage in hand and ask the hard questions but you President hold all the credentials to do just this. People of all nations hold you in high esteem and believe in what you stand for, you hold the key to change in so many ways. The world needs someone like you, someone who can effect real change, who can challenge old concepts about roots of poverty, someone who can challenge old and new economic dogmas which keep a huge percentage of the world population poor and hungry so that the rest of us may prosper way beyond our needs. In short, established myths can block our understanding and hence our ability to effect change.

# Nchedo Obi-Igweilo
*Ireland*

## Subject: CHILD LABOUR

Mr President, if you and I could recall our childhood you would agree with me that children feel happy and gain a sense of recognition when parents allow them to do voluntary chores. As a child I helped my mother in the kitchen or garden. It was my duty to sweep *nbala* – the family compound – while my sister fetched water and mother prepared breakfast.

In my village children are expected even today to sweep *amah* – the village square; to fetch firewood or water for lonely elderly people. Children share in farm work on weekends and holidays. I looked forward to looking after my grandmother's goats and sheep. I remember evenings sitting on a hilltop watching with them an African sunset; horizons splashed with hues of vibrant orange, reds and yellows against a deepening indigo sky.

For New Yam or Christmas feasts children in my village helped mothers in scrubbing and putting multiple designs around the mud house. During *harmattan* – the dry harvest season – children looked with delight to harvesting farm produce and setting up yam barns.

The lessons learned from these chores helped me in my adult life. Many who have had these experiences would agree that such models one to be responsible and active in one's community.

However, millions of children around the world, from the streets of Lagos, Kolkota, Manila and Cotonou to Rio de Janeiro and Nairobi today do not have these positive childhood experience as you and I had. Theirs are stories of abuses; of denied futures. Birthdays, which are a joy to you and I, are a nightmare to them.

Mr President, as I write to you, millions of children are being abused through child labour around the world. This is common in our cities. They work as street sellers or as cheap labourers in factories that produce our food, shoes and auto parts, or as sex workers, working under harsh conditions.

Their employers adopt them as slaves. Daily these children have little or no food, sleep and water. They have no time for leisure or education. Their "owners" – their employers – abuse them severely. They are traded like goats or trafficked from city to city, country to country.

Could you and I free them from the bondage called child labour? Should I continue to blame the parents of these children without taking universal action to protect them? If the EU and USA were able to end child labour in their territories, then yes we can universally end it. Many families today live in abject poverty, but with a shared responsibility we can end this. In most countries women have no rights to land or property; this too should be universally condemned.

Yes we can; you and I can free these children from the slave ship called child labour if we see child labour as a crime against humanity and place a UNO monitored ban on this criminal act. Through this we can make our world free of child labour where children are raped, drugged, murdered and trafficked. Yes we can!

# Richard Davies
*Ireland*

## Subject: WORLD HUNGER

In the last hundred years we have advanced more in the fields of science, technology and medicine than in all the previous centuries of human existence combined. We have put a man on the moon, split the atom, eliminated diseases such as small pox, developed vaccines for thousands of others, and created a world spanning communication network – otherwise known as the internet. Yet only a very privileged portion of the human population experiences the benefits of such advancements. The fact of the matter is that the majority lack the basic resources required to live any kind of long or comfortable life. Worse still, a significant portion of this impoverished majority lacks even the most basic human requirements such as proper food and water. Everyday, around 25,000 people die from starvation, while further millions will spend the night sleeping on empty stomachs. With the world population barrelling towards seven billion people, the question is simple: how are we supposed to feed all these people?

In 1968, Paul R. Ehrlich revived the issue of mass world hunger when he published *The Population Bomb*. Ehrlich asserted that mass overpopulation and a food shortage in the 1970s and 1980s would lead to a worldwide famine resulting in approximately 100 million deaths. The famine predicted by Ehrlich never occurred, partly because he failed to take into account the various advancements that were to occur in agricultural science and technology – advancements that allowed for better disease resistant and more sustainable crops that produced higher yields per square acre, making it possible to feed the millions who otherwise would have gone without.

The most prevalent and publicized individual in this field is Norman Borlaug, the father of the "Green Revolution". While Ehrlich and other pessimists were busy predicting the downfall of mankind, Borlaug and other agricultural scientists were busy exploring a combination of genetics, plant breeding, plant pathology, entomology, agronomy, soil science and cereal technology to better crop yields and feed the poor. In Mexico, Borlaug developed and refined a method of wheat production that almost single-handedly solved their food shortage crisis, millions of lives were saved. India became self-sustaining in cereal production as a result of the introduction of Borlaug's dwarf wheat varieties, saving further millions. In China, Borlaug's introduction of new rice strains allowed for more efficient and reliable food production thus saving further millions. Thanks to Borlaug's work, hundreds of millions – perhaps even billions – of lives have been spared from starvation. The lesson here is simple: provided that we are committed to investing the required amount of time, energy and money into the required areas, it is possible to feed the world's hungry. As Borlaug himself puts it: "You can't build a peaceful world on empty stomachs and human misery."

We need to understand that in order to get through the next 50 years it is going to take a global effort on a scale of never before seen proportions. The role of a person in a position of power such as yours is not to lead people; history has shown that people are generally suspicious and untrusting of power. The job is to encourage. It is important to let people know that it is not you who will instigate change, but themselves. The only way to get them to change is to get them to want to change.

Some could see the world economic crisis as the worst possible road block in the way of reducing world hunger; I believe that it is more of a sign. A sign showing us that the current manner in which we are spending money is totally unacceptable. It is a sign that the money spent investing in arms and obsolete fuel sources would perhaps be better spent investing in renewable energy resources, education, healthcare and – most importantly – in people.

The German writer Johann Wolfgang Van Goethe wrote that "nothing is worth more than this day". These words have never been more poignant than at the current point that we find ourselves in human history. Now is the time to invest in the things that we need rather than the things that we want. While the next 50 years are going to be shaky and at times scary, perhaps you could begin the first 4 on a positive note.

# Lisamarie Duffy
*Ireland*

**Subject: CHILD LABOUR**

I used to think I had big problems and now I realize just how trivial they are when I read about some of the inhumane way many people in the third world are treated. It just doesn't seem right that we live in such an unequal world, my biggest worry is waking up each morning and finding the right clothes to wear while for a girl my age living in the third world it may be that she simply survives that day, that she will not be beaten or raped, and she and her family will have enough food to see them through the day. It breaks my heart to think of girls my age forced into prostitution, or young children the same age as many of my cousins who are brain washed into becoming child soldiers. What sort of hope do these children have? For some it's too later, others we may be able to help but we must continuously think of new ways of supporting and setting up new charities. I am encouraging people in my area to do what they can, raising awareness alone is a big step, and it's only by highlighting this big problem that people will help out.

I want to thank you for taking the time out to read this letter. I hope to write again with an update on how my proposed project is going, however, I need help; if I am going to do it I want to do it right.

I hope all is going well for you and your wife and two daughters. I hope you have settled nicely into your new home. I think you are doing a great job!!

# James Bradshaw
*Ireland*

### Subject: WORLD HUNGER

No matter how tired and hungry he is, Joshua cannot stay in the shade any longer. By now his mother will have started to wonder what was taking him so long. The last few months had been especially hard on her; she had seen her sister emigrate, and witnessed her eldest son Anthony leaving school to try and find work so that the family would have food. She remembered how bright he was as a little boy, how happy he was leaving the house with Joshua every morning to walk to St. Martin's school just outside the village. Once he had told her that his dream was to be a doctor, but now he and his father spend their days travelling far and wide in search of employment. However, it had become increasingly hard to find work. Sometimes they would get hired temporarily on farms, but with so many Zimbabwean men competing for the same jobs, they were left idle more often than not. If they were working, the family had money to buy food. If they were not working, they went hungry. Just by looking at the almost empty bag of cornmeal in the family's kitchen, you could see that Anthony and his father had not found work in some time.

With thoughts of his mother fresh in his mind, Joshua slowly rises from the ground. His legs feel weak under him, and he has to use the tree as a support as he gets up. He picks up his basket, and begins the journey home. It has cooled down slightly while he was resting, but Joshua still feels very weak as he walks towards his beloved village. The basket is heavy, and drops of sweat roll down his forehead as he slowly makes his way home. All he can think about is the emptiness in his stomach and the food that he hopes will soon fill it.

He has not seen his Papa or Anthony in three days, and they are due back this evening. Joshua misses his brother's company and wishes he could return; however, he knows that it is more likely that they will be re-united in the fields than in the classroom. It doesn't matter how much his family wants him to be educated. While his future might not be as bright without an education, without food he might not have a future at all.

# Sarah Hooker

*Ireland*

### Subject: WORLD HUNGER

Africa has 922 million people, it occupies 14.2 per cent of the worlds surface and is made up of savannah, desert, lakes and peaks, people as varied as its ochre of its sands. It is a land of contrast, of angry beauty and sharp pain, laminated by a deep rooted hunger which contorts the faces of its children. Hunger is not confined to Africa neither should Africa be solely associated with it.

However it is here that I first found hunger, ingrained in its bothered soil and the lives of millions.

I grew up in Southern Africa, traveling between Lesotho, Mozambique, South Africa and Swaziland. This continent gave me the salty kiss of the Indian Ocean, the windy embrace of Cape Town and the passionate discourse of its people. I was molded by this journey, by this mélange of western influence and African thought. These places influenced my understanding of the afflictions which plagued them, and therefore are intrinsic to any contemplation of African hunger.

As a child growing up in the kingdom of Lesotho I struggled to define Hunger in relation to myself. I had arrived in Lesotho as part as a middle class family who had never known want. Why did some children eat, and some didn't? Why were cows more valuable than children? Why were there permanent beggars at the traffic lights who defended their turf by forming small gangs?

As a young girl of eight years, I sat with my caretaker as she ate plain *pap* with a thin watery sauce on our doorstep. I asked her why she didn't eat meat. She asked why I didn't give her meat. We sat, woman and child, as I realized that this is want. My education had begun.

If Lesotho was my introduction to hunger then Mozambique was my thesis. In Lesotho I questioned hunger because it was alien, whereas Mozambique taught me to ignore it because of the measure of its saturation.

Mozambique was a newly independent nation littered with crumbling Portuguese forts and untouched coral reefs. Faces painted with unfulfilled expectations ran after cars begging for cigarettes and sweets. Children played on dirt roads accented by the kisses of affectionate mines and men drank home grown brew in the shadows of mud huts.

I met old men who bowed their heads to me, just a girl, to ask for food so their families could survive another year and young men who knocked on our garden gate like clockwork to 'present' themselves for work. Any work. And, with a quick shake of my head, I would say no.

I looked at them with that look. That silent plead. That look that says I want to care but I cannot because if I care for you, I have to care for millions, and I cannot do that. That look that betrays a numbness because you are everywhere, every day. The look which says I have never been hungry so although I can try and understand, I never will.

Hunger pervaded and saturated my surroundings and I became immune to its affliction, to the suffering it extolled.

When I look back upon that time in Mozambique, I now think it was too easy to do that look. I imagine that is why it has caught on so well all over the world.

# Karen Mould

*Ireland*

## Subject: CLIMATE CHANGE

Ghulam Mohammad Panaullah, former research director of the Bangladesh Rice Research Institute (BRRI), stated: "The impact of climate change on agriculture is undeniable and will most certainly worsen if governments and donors fail to take appropriate steps right now."

This destruction doesn't just stop with Bangladesh. As well as many coastal Asian and African countries being effected there are also Central American countries also suffering as a consequence. Nicaragua is one of these Central American countries and dues to its location it is acknowledged to have many natural disasters. Hurricane Mitch struck Nicaragua in March 1998, and was considered to have caused the biggest devastation to the country to date. Unofficial reports talked of the hurricane dropping 50 inches of rain over the country, killing 3,800 people and leaving over 500,000 people homeless.

Nicaragua is considered to be the second poorest country in the Western hemisphere, with approximately 60 per cent of the nation working in agriculture. Nicaraguans, like many farmers in third world countries, predict seasonal changes for agriculture. Watching these seasonal changes allow these people to know when to plant, and when to harvest. As climate change begins to eradicate their seasons, crops are beginning to fail. Yet not only is erratic wet weather conditions destroying crops, it is also seeing dramatic droughts that mean river levels are lower then normal and affecting transport waterways between communities.

As the death toll continues to rise in the countries affected by climate change, can we not educate those in the first world. Ask these people as they sit in their central heated homes watching their 42" plasma TVs, ask those driving their 10 minute journey to work in their SUVs to consider those that live in conditions of poverty. Financial aid maybe a short-term solution but realistically climate change needs to be stemmed to allow these people to continue to farm and live self sufficiently.

# Paul Mayende
*Uganda*

**Subject:** CHILD LABOUR

**President Obama, make us jobless please**
I am sure Mr. President, many people in the developing world are looking forward to when millions of Americans will resume their jobs since this greatly impacts on aid and individual donations for

anti-retroviral therapy, education, clothing and other survival care of millions of children around the world.

Some of us are, however, requesting that attention is given to getting us out of the jobs we are doing since we are facing tasks beyond our abilities besides the abuse that we face each day. We are the children.

From where I am writing this letter, of the current 16.8 million children between 5-14 years in the country, 36 per cent are involved in child labour while 54 per cent experience early marriage which also comes with a package of labour.

We deserve education, Mr. President, and the reason is that we will use our education some day and become better people. Those of us heading households are doing these jobs so that we can cater for food, books, pens and clothes for ourselves and the young siblings but we are being overly exploited and abused, Mr. President.

As you focus on the need to create jobs for people in your country, we request that you use your God given position to help us out of this kind of employment. Let leaders from countries like mine know that you, Mr. President, detest the idea of using children as cheap labour. Let them know that they can not achieve development by brick making, quarrying and collecting empty old bottles all done by a bunch of kids. They can only achieve development by investing is us so that we acquire skills in how to make tiles from mud.

Mr. President, as you noted during your victory speech, if there is anybody who still doubts that as children we can be future engineers, doctors, lawyers and I hope presidents, then you are the answer.

You have a bigger platform Mr. President to address the world and request our leaders to implement policies that will enable us go to school, and protect us from exploitation. We are fully aware that still other children will be facing child labour and we can not end the suffering of the millions of child labourers now or tomorrow, but we are confident we can end it one day.

# Emma Green
*United Kingdom*

**Subject: CHILD LABOUR**

What happens to the rest of the children who don't receive this kind of help? It's the same old laborious work day in and day out! Children are little human beings who need the people who are higher up, those who waste their money on fighting wars and building new enterprises or meaningless statues. These people hold the key to children's futures and they are busy squandering their fortunes when there are human beings lives at risk each day. If all this money was saved these children could have brighter futures. If everyone got together and did their bit, millions of children would be better off. So, when you're putting your child to bed tonight think one of the most unimaginable thoughts a parent could have, what if your child was one of those millions slaving in a degrading job, and then think what you could do to stop that and help millions of others at the same time.

# Charlene Tola
*Ireland*

**SUBJECT: Child Labour**

Dear President Obama,
I am really happy for you as you won the elections. As you say 'change is what we believe'. My name is Bintou, I live in Pakistan

with my family. When I was four years old my parents were given about 800 Rupees about £12.70 in return for putting me to work in the village carpet factory. I wasn't the only child working in a factory there are about 150,000 children of my age working in factories. We are considered as good workers because of our small hands and we can work for about 14 hours a day and sometimes we do extra time without getting pay and no one can talk in case you get your hands burnt or be beaten very badly. My parents can't talk in case they won't get paid. During the work nobody is allowed to talk in case we make some mistakes in the patterns. I would love to go to school like children of other countries, be happy and play like them.

My parents can't afford to send me to school because they don't have any money and the farm they have is not working any more. The soil has become hard because of the Global warming. I am always praying to God to help me get out of this situation because the carpet factory man said my parents owe him 20,000 rupees. I am afraid I will have to work with the man all my entire life repaying the debt.

F is for Factory

# Mary Kinsella
*Ireland*

SUBJECT: **World Hunger**

This, Mr President, is a poem I have written about Sudan and I hope you will like it.

### Children of the African Sun

Children of the African sun,
See the world what it has done,
It has left you to die without a care,
With insects picking at your little hair.

Oh little child of the African sun,
You too should have your fun,
Living in a world that does not care.
And you are just lying there.

So let all governments take a look,
And see all the wicked things they have done,
To let a little child die in vain,
While they tell the world lies,
To play their war games.

# Concern Works

With more than 3,000 staff and 50 nationalities, Concern works in 28 of the world's poorest countries. We are supported by tens of thousands of people, as well as organisations and governments who all share the same concern.

Bound together by a shared humanity, we are a voice for change for the poorest of the poor, working with them in their communities and influencing decisions made at local, national and international levels that affect their lives, whether that's providing the know-how to build a well or the expertise and training to build a dam.

If we have learned anything in the 40 years since we started, it's that the little things can make a huge difference.

**In Niger**...through listening to parents and partnering school authorities, simple changes have been made so that school attendance and enrolment by girls has increased

**In Ethiopia**...our constant search for better ways led us to pioneer an innovative approach to treat malnutrition and young children. This approach, which we call Community Therapeutic Care (CTC) has proven so effective, it has been integrated into the World Health Organisation's nutrition guidelines

**In Pakistan**...Concern's local staff responded swiftly to a major earthquake in innovative ways that outside experts could not have, local knowledge and rapid action saves lives

Concern is often one of the first to arrive after a disaster and usually among the last to leave.

We stay until the people we work with have what it takes to get on with their lives.

None of us can change the past. But together we can make a better future. So that someday, everyone, everywhere, will have a decent standard of living. And every child will have the opportunity for a happy healthy life.

**Our Identity – Who We Are:**

Concern Worldwide is a non-governmental, international, humanitarian organisation dedicated to the reduction of suffering and working towards the ultimate elimination of extreme poverty in the world's poorest countries.

**Our Vision – For Change:**

A world where no one lives in poverty, fear or oppression; where all have access to a decent standard of living and the opportunities and choices essential to a long, healthy and creative life; a world where everyone is treated with dignity and respect.

**Our Mission – What We Do:**

Our mission is to help people living in extreme poverty achieve major improvements in their lives which last and spread without ongoing support from Concern.

**Our Values – What Guides Concern's Work:**

- **Extreme poverty must be targeted**. The quality of our overall endeavour must ultimately be measured by its contribution to the rapid elimination of the extreme form of poverty defined by the United Nations as "absolute poverty".

- **Respect for people comes first**. Poverty, no matter how extreme, reduces people's choices – not their competence and abilities. Respect is shown to all people with whom we engage; and in particular in our overseas work, we respect the integrity and dignity of the poor with whom we work.

- **Gender equality is a prerequisite for development**. The establishment of equality of opportunities between men and women is fundamental to both the achievement of fairness and to poverty elimination.

- **Development is a process, not a gift**. Development is a process that occurs in people and is achieved by them at their pace, either on their own or with outside facilitation. We hold as a fundamental tenet that people living in absolute poverty have, in varying degrees, personal capacities, local resources and external opportunities for their own self-development. It is imperative that our work builds on these resources.

- **Greater participation leads to greater commitment**. At home and overseas participation in decision-making leads to a greater and more sustained commitment to achieving developmental objectives. We believe in a high level and quality of participation by the poor in decision-making about development initiatives taken in partnership with them.

- **All governments have responsibility for poverty elimination**. Most of the poverty endured by countless numbers of people living in the developing world cannot be solved without changed national and international social, economic and political structures. Concern engages in advocacy to this end.

- **Emergencies call for rapid response**. We value the importance of being able to respond quickly, effectively and creatively to people unable to meet their basic needs, especially in sudden onset emergencies.

- **Democracy accelerates development**. Lack of equity in the distribution of power within and between societies retards the struggle against absolute poverty. Participatory democratic environments are the most favourable settings in which states, markets and people can together solve the problem of global poverty.

- **The environment must be respected**. The destruction of the environment poses a major threat to our target groups. We acknowledge the importance of protecting the earth's environment and the need to ensure that our development and advocacy work promotes the concept of environmental responsibility and the conservation of natural resources and their sustainable management.

- **Good stewardship ensures trust**. We hold money in trust for all of our donors and for their intended beneficiaries. This creates a responsibility to ensure we are accountable and to give value for money both to our donors and to our project participants.

- **Experience is the best teacher**. Our current policies, strategies and practices have been developed through our learning over the years. We value the ongoing process of learning and of participating in networks with other organisations to share experiences and learn from them.